LOCAL GOVERNMENT IN CRISIS

W. A. ROBSON

*Professor Emeritus in Public Administration
in the University of London*

LOCAL GOVERNMENT
IN CRISIS

London

GEORGE ALLEN & UNWIN LTD

RUSKIN HOUSE MUSEUM STREET

PRINTED IN GREAT BRITAIN
in 11 *on* 12 *point Bell type*
BY UNWIN BROTHERS LTD
WOKING AND LONDON

PREFACE

In 1931 I wrote *The Development of Local Government*. That book contained a discussion of the chief local govenment problems such as the organization of areas and authorities, the relations of the central departments to local authorities, the powers of local authorities, and municipal finance. In the preface I pointed out that the failure of successive Governments, Parliaments and the public to recognize the nature or even the existence of these problems had produced a situation of the utmost gravity to the local government system.

Much of the material on which my diagnosis and the conclusions were based was derived from a vast mass of facts which had come to light during a series of official enquiries which had taken place before 1930 and of which the Onslow Commission was the most important. In preparing the second edition of the book, published in 1947, it was not possible to bring all the factual material up to date because the necessary information was neither available nor easily obtainable. I therefore reprinted the original text with a minimum of revision but included a new Prologue containing an account of the more important events and trends which had occurred since the book had first appeared. I followed the same course in 1953, when a third edition was required. The Prologue bore the title of the present book.

With the passage of time the contents of the original book have become seriously out of date and some of it is no longer relevant. The Prologue, on the other hand, has become increasingly relevant as an analysis of the present condition of local government and a narrative of the events which has brought it about: so relevant, indeed, that it can now sustain an independent existence. I have therefore thoroughly revised the text and added new material which has almost doubled its length; and it is now presented as a short study in its own right. The title which it bore as a Prologue has been retained.

It is, unfortunately, all too appropriate as a description of the present situation in which local government now finds itself.

I wish to express my thanks to Mr Bruce Wood, B.Sc.(Econ.) who gave me valuable help in carrying out the research required for the preparation of this greatly enlarged and revised edition.

W. A. R.

January 1966

CONTENTS

LOCAL GOVERNMENT IN CRISIS

Local Government in Crisis

For the last thirty or forty years it has been abundantly clear that our system of municipal government was being subjected to a serious and potentially dangerous strain owing to the fact that it was confronted with tasks far greater than those which it was designed to perform. There are only two possible ways in which the strain can be relieved. One is to improve the structure so that it is capable of carrying an increased burden. The other is to transfer functions elsewhere and to avoid conferring on local authorities additional responsibilities which they might otherwise have been able to carry.

Everyone who cares for local government and values its essential contribution to the British democratic tradition would desire to see the former course adopted. Unfortunately, however, the tide has been flowing strongly in the opposite direction—just how strongly I shall show in the following pages.

A visitor to England at almost any time during the past twenty years might well have come to believe that the reform of local government was moving strongly forward. The question of municipal reorganization has been under almost continuous discussion in official circles since the closing years of the Second World War. The reason, however, is not because either local councillors or local government officers or the local authority associations desire reform, but because they fear that if they do not make proposals reform may be carried too far. In consequence, the reform movement has been a movement to prevent or slow down reform.

Until the appointment of the Maud Committee on People in Local Government in 1964 it has been generally assumed that only members or officers of local authorities, or their associations, were competent to express sound views on matters of reconstruction; and hence all discussion and negotiation has been confined to a narrow circle of persons with a special bias or associations with a vested interest. The Herbert Commission on Local Government in Greater London broke through this narrow ring with notable results, and the Maud Committee is known to be using the services of the Social Survey of the Central Office of Information to discover the views of ordinary citizens towards local government.

A belated recognition that all is not well with local government was shown by the request of the four main local authority associations to the Minister of Housing and Local Government early in 1964 to appoint two committees to inquire into the personnel engaged in local government. The Minister (Sir Keith Joseph) acceded to this request, and the Maud and Mallaby Committees were in due course set up. The terms of reference of the Maud Committee are 'to consider in the light of modern conditions how local government might best continue to attract and retain people (both elected representatives and principal officers) of the calibre necessary to ensure its maximum effectiveness'. The Mallaby Committee was asked 'to consider the existing methods of recruiting local government officers and of using them; and what changes might help local authorities to get the best possible service and help their officers to give it'.

No one would wish to discourage such well-intentioned efforts as these; but the Maud Committee is asked to deal with the consequences of a deep-seated malaise without being able to examine and pronounce on its fundamental causes. Local government is suffering from a momentum of decline comparable to that which afflicted the coal industry in the years between, say, 1920 and 1950. An inquiry into the question of whether the coal industry was attracting men of the right quality in, say, 1945 could only have returned a negative answer. The causes were complex. It would have been impossible to devise a means of recruiting men of greater ability, energy and knowledge to the industry without first diagnosing the maladies from which the industry was suffering and then finding ways to cure them. To replace a momentum of decline by a momentum of advance is an extremely difficult and complex operation in any sphere of activity.

A somewhat similar situation, *mutatis mutandis*, exists in local government today. I do not suggest that nothing can be done to improve the quality of councillors and local government officers in present circumstances. But any substantial improvement will demand far-reaching changes in the structure and the finance of local government, the relations of local authorities with central departments, and the powers entrusted to local councils. That is what this book is about.

I

THE LOSS OF MUNICIPAL FUNCTIONS

I. THE REGULATION OF PASSENGER ROAD SERVICES

The most conspicuous tendency in recent years has been the removal of functions from local government control. In 1930 the licensing of passenger road services was taken away by the Road Traffic Act from local authorities and given to the traffic commissioners set up in twelve large regions.[1] The licensing authorities are appointed by the Minister of Transport and are subject to his general directions. The chairman of each body is a full-time officer who holds office during Her Majesty's pleasure. The other two members are drawn from two panels, one nominated by the county councils and the other by the county boroughs, non-county boroughs and urban districts in the region concerned. A connection with local government is maintained through the personnel of these panels, but the regulation of motorbuses and coaches has ceased to be a local government service. A person appointed from one of the panels may continue to serve after he has ceased to be a member of the local authority which nominated him; and he is in any event in no way responsible to the local council for the decisions of the licensing authority.[2]

II. TRUNK ROADS

In 1936, 3,500 miles of trunk road, forming part of the national system of routes for through traffic, were transferred from the

[1] The number has now been reduced to eleven, but the traffic area for Scotland has been divided into two sub-areas. See Road Traffic Act, 1960, S. 119.

[2] For the Metropolitan traffic area there is a single commissioner. For a discussion of this and other Administrative Tribunals see W. A. Robson: *Justice and Administrative Law* (3rd ed.) ch. 3; R. M. Cushman: *The Independent Regulatory Commissions*, p. 543 et seq.

local highway authorities to the Minister of Transport, who was henceforth made entirely responsible for their maintenance, repair and improvement. This change did not affect roads in county boroughs or the county of London. In 1946 a further long list of main highways, comprising an additional 3,000 miles of trunk routes, was transferred to the central government. Furthermore, the Minister is now authorised to declare any road to be a trunk road by order and thus bring it within the system of national routes under his control. Moreover, the main highways in the county boroughs and the former county of London are no longer excluded from the national routes under the Minister.[1] By 1964 6,401 miles of main highways had been transferred to the Minister of Transport and 1,946 miles to the Secretary of State for Scotland.

This legislation provides for a division of duties between the Minister of Transport and the former highway authorities. The Minister may delegate functions in respect of the national routes to county borough or county councils, and he does so on a liberal scale; but this does not affect the basic fact that responsibility for the principal roads of the country has passed from local authorities to the central government.

III. HOSPITALS

The loss of the hospital service was a far more serious blow to local government than roads. The abolition of the boards of guardians in 1929 and the transfer of their functions and property to the county and county borough councils had made local authorities responsible for a large majority of the hospitals. The total accommodation provided by them was 355,000 beds in 1,545 hospitals, out of a total of 504,000 beds in 2,688 hospitals taken over by the Ministry of Health under the National Health Service Act, 1946. The municipal hospital service was, moreover, an expanding service both as regards the scope of the treatment that it offered and the sections of the community for which it catered. It was no longer associated with

---

[1] Trunk Roads Acts, 1936 and 1946.

the Poor Law. It was meeting the needs of an ever-widening circle of citizens and substantial improvements were being effected in regard to the medical service, buildings, equipment, management, and staffing arrangements. Hospital administration was, indeed, one of the services in which large developments might with some confidence have been predicted in the municipal sphere until 1946. Then suddenly, local authorities were deprived of the whole mass of their hospitals at one stroke. It was a shattering blow to local government. The London County Council, to take the outstanding instance, was the largest hospital authority in the world. It ceased to be a hospital authority at all. The only contact which local authorities continue to have with this supremely important part of the National Health Service is that the Regional Hospital Boards must include among their members 'persons appointed after consultation with the local health authorities in the area'.[1] These persons form only one out of four categories of persons who are to be included on the boards. They need not be councillors, aldermen or officers of local authorities. They do not serve in a representative capacity and are appointed by the Minister. The Regional Hospital Boards appoint Hospital Management Committees for the hospitals in their region and here again the members include persons appointed after consultation with the appropriate local health authorities. The local government influence over the hospital service has thus been so attenuated and diluted that it is reduced to almost negligible proportions.

IV. PUBLIC ASSISTANCE

Other changes of great significance have taken place in the social services. The Unemployment Act, 1934, transferred to the Assistance Board responsibility for the able-bodied unemployed who had exhausted their rights to unemployment insurance benefit. In 1940 the supplementation of old age and widows pensions, which had previously fallen on the local authorities, was vested in the Assistance Board. The National Assistance Act, 1948, which is a much more compre-

[1] National Health Service Act, 1946. Third Schedule. Part 1.

hensive measure, superseded and repealed the earlier legislation, including the Poor Law. It renamed the Assistance Board the National Assistance Board, and gave it the duty of relieving destitution and of assisting persons in need, which local authorities had possessed since the days of the Elizabethan Poor Law.

Local authorities no longer exercise any powers relating to the payment of money to persons in need, and their functions consist of providing services in kind for certain categories of persons. Thus, they must provide accommodation for those who, by reason of age, infirmity or other circumstances, require care and attention which they could not otherwise obtain. They must also provide accommodation for those rendered temporarily homeless by an emergency or other circumstances. Persons who use the accommodation are normally required to pay standard charges, which may be reduced in cases of need. In addition, the local authorities must maintain certain welfare services for physically handicapped persons in need of them. Most of the institutional forms of assistance available to those in need are now given under the National Health Service or as part of the ordinary public health or education services. The National Assistance Board discharges its functions through its own local offices. The responsibilities left to local authorities under the new system are thus much narrower in scope and far less important in magnitude than those they fulfilled under either the old Poor Law or the later system of public assistance.

V. VALUATION AND ASSESSMENT FOR RATING

The system of local rates evolved historically from the Elizabethan Poor Law, which introduced a poor rate in each parish to finance the relief of destitution. In course of time the rates became the sole instrument of local taxation by means of which revenue was provided for all the services of local authorities. The rating system was gradually reformed and extended, notably in 1925, when the Rating and Valuation Act enlarged the rating areas, and again in 1929 when public assistance was transferred from the boards of guardians to the county and county borough councils. Despite many changes, the whole business of valuation, assessment and collection of rates was administered entirely by local authorities for nearly 350 years.

In 1948, however, an important change occurred which had nothing to do with the transfer of public assistance functions from local authorities to a national organ. The Local Government Act, 1948, introduced a new grant known as the Exchequer Equalization grant to take the place of the former block grant; and in the course of making this change, Parliament transferred the task of valuing property for rating purposes from local authorities to the Inland Revenue. The principle underlying the Equalization grant was that the Exchequer became, in effect, a ratepayer of a local authority to the extent that the latter had a deficiency in rateable value per head compared with the average for the whole country. The Exchequer paid rates on that amount at the appropriate rate in the £ for that area; and each local authority which qualified for the grant received from national funds a proportion of the expenditure which would otherwise have fallen on the rates.

The Equalization grant gave the Exchequer a direct interest in the valuation of property for rating, since entitlement to grant depended on whether a local authority was or was not below the national average for the whole country as regards the rateable value per head of its weighted population. There had for long been considerable differences in the standard of valuation applied to property in different areas; and sometimes these differences were due to deliberate attempts to conceal the full extent of the differences in rateable value between different areas: as, for example, when a wealthy local authority preferred to levy a high rate on under-valued property rather than a lower rate on a more accurate valuation. This was the Treasury's justification for removing the process of valuation entirely from the sphere of local government. The Rate Deficiency Grant which has replaced the Equalization Grant has a similar aim and, like its predecessor, requires a uniform system of valuation for the whole country.

If we are to interpret aright the movement towards centralization whose progress we are here recording, we must remember that reasons can always be adduced for almost any policy;

and some of the reasons for centralization will seem to be good reasons if we consider each step in isolation, especially if we do not contemplate the total effect on the system of local government of a series of losses of power, independence and responsibility.

II

THE LOSS OF PUBLIC UTILITIES

I. PASSENGER ROAD TRANSPORT SERVICES

In the field of public utilities some spectacular changes have occurred and others are threatened. The case of transport may be considered first.

Before the Second World War there were ninety-five local authorities operating motor-bus and motor-coach services, in addition to sixty-seven tramway and thirty-nine trolley-bus undertakings, most of which were in the hands of borough councils. At the end of 1950–51 local authorities owned 14,596 motor-buses, 2,509 trolley-buses and 3,803 trams.

Under the Transport Act, 1947, which nationalized inland transport, all passenger road services, whether municipal or commercial, were liable to be taken away from their owners and formed into new undertakings under entirely different management. The now defunct British Transport Commission was authorized to prepare and submit to the Minister of Transport schemes for passenger road services covering specified areas. A scheme might establish or specify the body or bodies which were to provide services within the area, and it could designate the bodies to acquire and administer the undertaking. The British Transport Commission might name itself as the operating body, either alone or in conjunction with other organs.

The British Transport Commission was required by the Act of 1947 to review as soon as possible the passenger road transport services operating in Great Britain with a view to deciding for which areas schemes were to be prepared. Little progress was made in carrying out these provisions of the Act and in July, 1951, Mr Barnes, then Minister of Transport, complained of the number of local authorities which had resisted area schemes. He expressed his disappointment at the slow progress being made with area road passenger schemes which, he said, could only materialize through local consent and local option.[1] *Cet animal est très méchant, quand on l'attaque, il se defend!*

The Transport Act, 1953, repealed these and other provisions of the 1947 Act affecting road transport; and the threat to municipal undertakings was thereby removed for the time being. But the prospect that local authorities will remain in undisturbed possession of their local transport services is a slender one; for the issue between the parties is that of nationalization versus profit-making enterprise, and the fate of municipal trading services is a mere incident of that controversy. Thus, the Conservative Government which introduced the 1953 Act were fundamentally interested in restoring road haulage and passenger services to private ownership; it happened almost by accident that in the process of repealing the provisions of the Transport Act, 1947, which authorized the Transport Commission to expropriate road haulage or passenger services in private ownership, the threat to municipally owned and operated passenger services was also removed. But no political party has advocated or defended municipal enterprise in connection with transport services or any other utility functions. Hence, local authority interests are a mere pawn in the struggle over nationalization. This applies not only to road passenger services but also to ports, which were dealt with in a somewhat similar manner by the Transport Act, 1947, and the denationalizing Act of 1953.

II. WATER SUPPLY

At the present time about 80 per cent of the water supply industry is municipally owned. Most of the undertakings are run directly by local authorities, while some are administered by boards controlled by municipal councils. The remaining 20 per cent of the industry is owned and operated by commercial companies. In Scotland all water undertakings are in municipal operation.

---

[1] *Municipal Year Book*, 1953, p. 438.

THE LOSS OF PUBLIC UTILITIES

The Labour Party in its 1964 Election Manifesto announced its intention of nationalizing the water supply industry. The detailed proposals have not yet been made public but it will be surprising if these do not involve the removal of this basic public utility from the sphere of local government. Mr Harold Wilson stated that the responsibilities of the Minister of Land and Natural Resources would include responsibility for reorganizing the water supply industry under full public ownership.

III. ELECTRICITY SUPPLY

Until 1947 the generation of electricity had been organized for the previous twenty years on a national basis by the joint efforts of the Electricity Commission and the Central Electricity Board. The generating stations were connected with a nation-wide grid, into which electricity is poured and from which supplies were drawn by authorized undertakers for distribution in detail. The distribution side of electricity supply was unaffected by the extensive progress introduced on the generating side by the Electricity Supply Act, 1926; and it had for long been recognized that sweeping reforms were needed.

About two-thirds of the electricity supply industry was owned and operated by local authorities, the remainder being in the hands of commercial companies. Municipal corporations owned nearly 60 per cent of the total capital sunk in the industry before 1947; they supplied 67·8 per cent of the consumers and disposed of 63 per cent of the total units supplied excluding bulk supplies. Local authorities had expended capital sums amounting to £330m, compared with £230m by the companies.

The performance of local authorities in this field compared on the whole favourably with that of the companies. The average price per unit charged by them for lighting, heating and cooking purposes was substantially lower; and they had also embarked to a much larger extent on schemes for assisted wiring and for the simple hire of apparatus at very low rentals.[1]

[1] For details see the memorandum on 'The Contribution of Local Authorities to the Development of the Electricity Supply Industry', issued by the Incorporated Municipal Electrical Association, pp. 5–6.

Proper consideration of local conditions is essential if the electricity supply industry is to be developed on economical and efficient lines and suitable provision made for meeting individual needs. The Municipal Electrical Association justly claimed that 'a type of organization which under efficient technical and financial direction places the consumer first, and is under local control, so that appropriate decisions may be promptly taken and implemented, will provide the cheapest and most satisfactory service'. They therefore contended that the needs of the community would best be served and the supply of electricity made available to the greatest number of consumers at the lowest possible cost, if the vigorous extension and development of local authority ownership were brought about.[1] The Association regarded with apprehension the prospect of electricity supply being transferred from municipal and company undertakings either to ad hoc bodies or to a national organ. Municipal ownership, they declared, is not incompatible with operation by joint boards covering wide areas; but the IMEA made no proposals for the organization of local authorities on a larger scale.

The Electricity Act, 1947, showed how well-founded were the fears of the Association. Under that measure and subsequent amending legislation the generation of electricity passed to a central body called the Central Electricity Generating Board and distribution was entrusted to twelve regional organs called Area Electricity Boards. The Electricity Council was established in 1957 to bring together the generating and the distributing organs. Thus, electricity supply has been wholly removed from the sphere of local government. The only remaining link is that each Area Electricity Board, the members of which are appointed by the Minister of Power, must be composed of persons who have had experience of and shown capacity in local government, industrial, commercial or financial matters, applied science, administration, or the organization of workers.

In each area a Consultative Council is set up, consisting of

---

[1] For details see the memorandum on 'The Contribution of Local Authorities to the Development of the Electricity Supply Industry', issued by the Incorporated Municipal Electrical Association, p. 7.

between twenty and thirty persons. Between two-fifths and three-fifths of the members are appointed by the Minister from a panel nominated by local authorities in the area. The Consultative Councils, as their name implies, are merely advisory bodies. They can consider any matter touching the distribution of electricity in the area, including tariffs and the improvement of services or facilities; they can hear complaints by consumers or discuss questions referred to them by the Area Board. They have a right to be informed of the Area Board's general plans and arrangements; and they in turn must report their conclusions to the Area Board or to the Central Electricity Generating Board. If the Board takes no action to implement their recommendations, or to remedy a defect or to meet criticism made by a Consultative Council, the latter, after consulting the Board, can make representations to the Electricity Council or ultimately the Minister of Power.[1]

IV. GAS UNDERTAKINGS

A similar situation existed in the gas supply industry, except that the share of the industry in the hands of local authorities was only about 37 per cent. The Gas Act, 1948, deprived 274 councils of their municipal gas undertakings and transferred them to twelve public corporations known as Area Gas Boards. The gas boards cover very large regions and are subject to a limited degree of co-ordination and supervision by the Gas Council. No compensation was paid to local authorities for the acquisition of their gas or electricity undertakings. They were merely relieved of responsibility for the interest and sinking fund charges in respect of any outstanding loans on their undertakings. The only other sums payable to them were £2½m to make up for the losses caused by severance of the gas undertakings, and £5m for the severance of the electricity undertakings.

Prior to this legislation being passed great apprehension was felt by local authorities concerning the future of the gas

[1] For a full account of the nationalized industries see my book *Nationalized Industry and Public Ownership* (2nd edition) Allen & Unwin, 1962.

industry and also for that matter of public utilities generally. At a conference on local government held by the Association of Municipal Corporations at Eastbourne on September 25 and 26, 1946, a paper was presented for discussion at the first session of the conference by Councillor C. E. P. Stott of Manchester on 'The Gas Industry in Relation to Local Government'.[1] Councillor Stott shared the view of the Labour Government that gas should be publicly owned, but he desired to see the two-thirds share of the industry then in private hands placed under the ownership and operation of local authorities or combinations of local authorities. 'I agree', he said, 'that there must be regional organization and co-ordination on a national basis, but this is a minor issue compared with the bigger one of local or national ownership.'

Councillor Stott pointed out that if nationalization meant that the industry was to be centralized or placed under the control of nominated persons forming a committee or board, then the gas undertakings would become insensitive to public requirements and remote from the healthy influence of public opinion. The share of the industry run by municipalities, he declared, had been operated competently by them and they were equally competent to administer the undertakings then owned by companies.

V. DEMOCRATIC CONTROL OF PUBLIC UTILITIES

Councillor Stott placed the whole subject against a background of broad political principle. 'Our conception of democracy', he declared, 'is the right of the individual freely to select the person whom he or she desired to administer or control local or national services. The test should be the ability to attach responsibility to an elected person, and I view with considerable trepidation the growth of such organization as the London Passenger Transport Board, not because of defects in their services, but because of the remoteness of the control over

[1] See Report of Proceedings issued by the Association of Municipal Corporations, p. 30.

them.'[1] The idea that Parliament can exercise control is, he continued, illusory. Parliament is not designed to administer services or to control effectively their administration and it cannot exercise that degree of continuous supervision over public utilities that is required if they are to be subject to the popular will.

The speaker also dismissed the idea that advisory committees are an adequate means of bridging the gap between municipal authorities and independent public corporations. It is possible, Councillor Stott warned his colleagues, that we shall be offered advisory panels and told that our function is to assist administrators to maintain contact with the body of consumers. 'We shall have place without responsibility and fool the public into believing that they have some measure of association with the industry. It is a seductive proposition—a shadow for the substance; an instrument denuded of power; a complete reversal of present practice, in which we receive advice from our technical staff and determine policy under their considerable influence. The possibility of the future is that we shall occupy the role of endeavouring to influence the policy of our masters.' For these reasons, Councillor Stott declared that any step attempting to destroy or limit the authority of local government in this field would be a retrograde step which should be resisted.

The position of local authorities under the nationalization schemes applied to gas and electricity is exactly what Councillor Stott warned his colleagues it would become: they have place without responsibility.

[1] See Report of Proceedings issued by the Association of Municipal Corporations, p. 30. The London Passenger Transport Board is now known as London Transport.

III

SOCIALIST BELIEF IN
MUNICIPAL TRADING

A movement for the widest possible extension of municipal trading services was for long an outstanding feature of the Socialist movement in England from the end of the nineteenth century. The early Fabians were known as 'gas and water socialists' because they advocated the ownership by local authorities of gas, water, electricity, street transport and other public utilities as an essential part of their programme. Bernard Shaw's book, *The Commonsense of Municipal Trading*, indicates the importance given to the matter by a leading thinker. Sidney and Beatrice Webb stated that there were 'obvious reasons why many industries and services have to be municipalized rather than nationalized'.[1] In their view the case for local administration of such functions rests primarily on the consciousness, among the inhabitants of a given area, of a sense of neighbourhood and of common needs differing from those of other localities; and on the facility with which members of a local community can take counsel together for the purpose of determining and developing their environment. The residents in a given area, the Webbs pointed out, must necessarily use the same drainage system, the same water supply, the same artificial sources of light and heat, the same educational and medical institutions, the same libraries, the same parks and open spaces, and the same organization of local transport. This tie of neighbourhood 'influences in a thousand unforeseen ways the nature of the administration. In the characteristic municipal industries and services producer and consumer are very near together, and automatically aware of each other.'[2]

For these reasons the Webbs declared that there was

[1] *A Constitution for the Socialist Commonwealth of Great Britain*, p. 213.
[2] *Ibid.*, p. 213.

practically no limit to the number and range of the industries and services that might with advantage be undertaken by local authorities.[1] A few great industries and services, such as railways and canals, afforestation, the supply of coal and oil, the generation of electricity and probably banking and insurance, would be undertaken by the central government. At the other end of the scale would be the provision of commodities for household consumption by the Co-operative Movement. In between would come an immense field of industrial enterprise which local authorities could undertake. 'It is, of course, easy to contemplate', they wrote 'the universal provision by our local authorities of water, gas and (so far as its distribution is concerned) electricity; of such local transport as tramways, omnibuses, ferries and river services. . . .'[2] It may well prove to be the case, they asserted, that in a Socialist Commonwealth as much as one-half of the entire range of industries and services would fall within the sphere of local government.[3]

These confident predictions conflict strangely with the course of events under the direction of Labour Ministers, many of whom acquired their Socialist beliefs from the teaching of the Webbs and other leading Fabians. In place of the great increase of industrial and distributive undertakings and social services which, it was prophesied, would expand the sphere of local government, we observe the removal from local authorities both of public utilities and essential social services.

[1] *A Constitution for the Socialist Commonwealth of Great Britain*, p. 236.
[2] *Ibid.*, p. 237.   [3] *Ibid.*, p. 238.

IV

NEW TOWNS

Local government is also suffering from being by-passed in respect of new functions. An outstanding example is the building of new towns, which now forms one of the most imaginative and promising features of Britain's reconstruction and development programme. The Reith Committee recommended that local authorities should be permitted to initiate the creation of new towns if they desired to do so. The Committee had in mind particularly the case where a large town, in order to carry out redevelopment on sound lines, needs to displace part of its population and industry and this can best be effected by building a new town or effecting a major extension to an existing small town.[1] These recommendations were not accepted by the Government and the New Towns Act, 1946, makes no provision for development corporations to be sponsored by local authorities. In consequence the new towns are being built without the participation of local authorities.

[1] Interim Report of the New Towns Committee. Cmd. 6759/1946. para. 9 (6).

V

SOME LOCAL GOVERNMENT GAINS

The trend has not been entirely in one direction, and local authorities have gained a few services to offset these staggering losses of power and responsibility. They are authorized by the Civic Restaurants Act, 1947, to provide and administer restaurants and to supply meals to the public, thus continuing the cheap meals service inaugurated by British Restaurants during the Second World War.

One would have expected local authorities to have shown great interest and enthusiasm in developing this service, remembering the unfavourable contrast presented in the past between the excellent municipal cafés and flourishing civic restaurants in many continental cities and the total lack of any comparable municipal enterprise in this country where local authorities had no legal power. Actually, however, we find less and less use being made of the Civic Restaurants Act. Thus, in July 1945, as many as 1,578 civic restaurants were in operation. By August 1948, the number had diminished to 937. In August, 1950, it was 474, and in April 1952 there were only 257. Since then there appears to have been a continuous decline in the meals served by civic restaurants judging by their revenue income, which remained almost unchanged at £1·8m between 1954–55 and 1962–63, a period in which there was a heavy increase in the price of meals. The fluctuations in revenue during this decade were slight. The lowest figure was £1·6m in 1957–58 and the highest £1·9m in 1961–62. There has therefore either been a reduction in the number of civic restaurants or a decline in their business.[1] We cannot explain the dwindling of this service by the statutory provision requiring civic restaurants to pay their way, for there is no reason what-

[1] For the annual figures see Local Government Financial Statistics 1954–55 to 1962–63.

29

ever why municipal restaurants and cafés should not be self-supporting.

The town and country planning powers of county councils and county borough councils were enlarged by the Town and Country Planning Act, 1947, and the Town Development Act, 1952. A further extension of their interests and jurisdiction was brought about by the National Parks and Access to the Countryside Act, 1949, in regard to the management of national parks, nature reserves, and the provision of rural amenities generally.

The major local authorities were given much wider powers and duties of looking after children deprived of a normal home life by the Children Act, 1948. A new emphasis was placed on what had been a neglected and badly organised service by the Curtis Report and its legislative sequel. County and county borough councils now have a positive duty to receive and care for orphans, deserted children, or those whose parents are prevented by disease or some other cause from giving them a proper home and upbringing.

The Clean Air Act, 1956, allows local authorities to establish smoke control areas. The Mental Health Act, 1959, envisages less use of hospitals for mentally ill persons and the development of community care, assisted by home visiting, training centres and hostels. These can all be provided by local health authorities under the Act. The National Assistance Act was amended in 1962 to enable county and county borough councils to provide meals and recreation for old people instead of using voluntary bodies for this purpose. Parish councils were authorised by the Parish Councils Act, 1957, to construct roadside seats and shelters, to light roads and public places, to provide parking accommodation for cycles and motor-cycles (but not for motor-cars or lorries!), and even to purchase a public clock for the village.

An important provision of the Local Government Act, 1948, permits local authorities to provide and support entertainment and the arts, and thereby to help people to make better use of their leisure time.[1] About thirty municipal corporations own

---

[1] For an excellent account of the use made of these and analogous powers in Greater London, see S. K. Ruck: *Municipal Entertainment and the Arts in Greater London.* (George Allen & Unwin, 1965.)

theatres, some of them being leased to a trust on which in a few instances the local authority is represented. There are about thirty-five theatre building projects by local authorities now in progress or approved; some of them are being carried out by municipal corporations which already own theatres, such as Bristol and Scunthorpe, others by town councils which have not previously been active supporters of the live theatre.[1]

Several attempts have been made to discover the extent to which local authorities have made use of the powers conferred on them by the 1948 Act. The most comprehensive report is the survey published by the Institute of Municipal Entertainment in April 1964. This contains a summary of expenditure for the two years 1947–48 and 1961–62; and gives detailed information of the entertainments provided or assisted by individual local authorities in the latter year. Information was sought by questionnaire from all county borough councils, borough councils and urban district councils. Replies were not received from 148 authorities, but most of these were very small and their contribution is unlikely to have significantly affected the total picture; 311 local authorities furnished a nil return.

The gross expenditure for 1961–62 under this heading was £7·4m compared with £2·8m in 1947–48. This is a surprisingly small increase considering the heavy fall in the value of money. The gross income was £2·4m in 1947–48 and £4·8m in 1961–62, leaving net expenditure at £370,442 in 1947–48 and £2,549,186 in 1961–62.

The authorized expenditure, after deducting receipts, may not exceed the product of a sixpenny rate. The net expenditure of the 535 urban authorities covered by the survey for the year 1961–62 was slightly in excess of a penny rate—scarcely a lavish provision. This, of course, was the average, and some local authorities spent much more. The Urban District Council of Ebbw Vale, for example, spent a sum equal to the proceeds of a 5·9d rate, thus almost reaching the legal limit.

---

[1] A conference on Civic Theatres was held in London at County Hall on February 24–25, 1965, organized jointly by the Association of Municipal Corporations and the Theatres Advisory Council. A full account of the proceedings and much useful information is printed in *The Municipal Review*, April 1965 and May 1965.

A very wide range of artistic activities are supported or assisted by local authorities. They include a considerable number of excellent repertory theatre companies, such as the Old Vic Company at Bristol and the theatres at Coventry and Nottingham.

The drama is only one item out of many supported by local authorities. Choral societies, concerts, music festivals, folk-dancing, puppet shows, mock parliaments, musical comedies, opera, pantomime, regattas, pageants, ballet, fairs and circuses, film shows, firework displays, sports meetings, tennis and bowls competitions, are among the multifarious forms of recreation or entertainment which local authorities now provide. Life in Britain is richer, gayer, and more colourful because of these activities.

When due allowance has been made for these and other gains, it is scarcely open to doubt that since the end of World War Two local government has on balance emerged weakened and diminished in stature. Local authorities have lost nearly all their trading services, and they are scarcely playing even second fiddle in the administration of the health service or public assistance.

Equally serious is the fact that the experimental legislation by means of Private Bills which formerly played so large a part in the initiation of new activities by the more enterprising authorities in public health and other fields has dwindled to negligible proportions. Government departments have an important influence on Parliamentary decisions in these matters, and governments nowadays look with suspicion and distrust on any deviations from the norm. So, as Professor Keith-Lucas truly observes, 'the frontiers of local municipal enterprise have almost ceased to expand, and local government has lost the excitement and the opportunities that it once had'.[1]

[1] 'The too-narrow Powers of Council', p. 31 in *Local Government Today and Tomorrow*, Ed. Dudley Lofts.

VI

THE TRANSFER OF POWERS FROM COUNTY DISTRICTS TO COUNTY COUNCILS

Within the framework of local government significant changes have taken place. Power and responsibility have shifted from the county district councils to the county councils. The Education Act, 1944, made county councils and county boroughs local education authorities for all purposes and eliminated the boroughs and urban districts which were formerly responsible in many areas for elementary education only. Under the present system the county council may appoint divisional executives to exercise specified functions relating to primary and secondary education. Provision is also made for a borough or urban district which satisfies certain conditions to be an excepted district and to have its own scheme of divisional administration. The district council then has the right to exercise functions delegated by the county council.[1]

The Police Act, 1946, abolished 47 police forces maintained by non-county boroughs and transferred the power previously possessed by those boroughs to the county police authorities.[2] Formerly, fire brigades were provided by county district councils until they were taken over by the central government during the Second World War. The Fire Services Act, 1947, returned the fire brigades to local authorities, but placed them in the hands of the county boroughs and county councils. The Town and Country Planning Act, 1947, transferred planning powers from county district councils to county councils. Under the National Health Service Act, 1946, county boroughs and county councils are made local health authorities, and in consequence county district councils have lost their powers in regard

---

[1] Education Act, 1944. First Schedule. Part III. For fuller details see *post* p. 35–6.
[2] Police Act, 1946, Section I.

to maternity and child welfare, ambulances, midwives, notification of births, vaccination and immunization, and various other matters.[1]

Thus, county district councils have since 1944 ceased to be local authorities for education, police, fire services, town and country planning, and health services. Housing is now the only service of major importance in which they play an independent role. In regard to all these other functions they have either been superseded entirely by the county councils or relegated to a subordinate position as the recipient of delegated powers and working under close supervision and control by the county council as regards policy and finance.

[1] National Health Service Act, 1946, Part III and Tenth Schedule.

VII

DELEGATION OF POWERS
TO DISTRICT COUNCILS

Before the Second World War there was very little delegation in local government. The Local Government Acts of 1888 and 1894 authorised county councils to delegate their functions to district councils; and from the beginning of the present century legislation dealing with specific services, such as midwives, small holdings, the housing of rural workers and the registration of nursing homes contained similar provisions, but little or no use was made of these powers.[1] The Local Government Act, 1929, which permitted county councils to delegate the right to maintain county roads to a district council at county expense, replaced an earlier nineteenth-century enactment which enabled urban authorities to claim the right to perform these functions.

Delegation became a matter of substantial importance with the passing of the Education Act, 1944, which introduced delegation as a means of compensating county district councils (which had formerly been 'Part III authorities') for the loss of their powers to provide elementary schools. This led to the divisional executives and the excepted districts.

The excepted districts were urban county districts with a population of 60,000 or more on June 30, 1939, or with an elementary school population of 7,000 and over on March 31, 1939. Areas which did not satisfy these conditions could be designated special districts by the Minister of Education. No provision was made for new excepted districts to be created until the Local Government Act, 1958 was passed. This provides that towns which have subsequently reached the 60,000

[1] For details see Peter G. Richards: *Delegation in Local Government*, Allen & Unwin, 1956, Chapter 2.

population level shall become excepted districts. Moreover, the position is to be reviewed at specified intervals of time.

Initially forty-four excepted districts came into existence, of which no fewer than sixteen were in Middlesex. They included Luton and Solihull, which have recently become county boroughs. The abolition of the Middlesex County Council as part of the reform of Greater London government has reduced the number of excepted districts to thirty-three. The great majority of them are non-county boroughs.

The essential features of delegation are that control of policy and of finance rests with the county council, and staff working in the delegated service are county employees with minor exceptions.[1] Within this basic framework of control the amount of discretion which is given to the district council varies immensely. The Ministry of Education, in a circular which was clearly defensive in tone, recognized that 'responsibility for broad educational policy, finance and general standards of provision must always remain with the county authority'. At the other end of the scale, many important duties and powers have been given to the managers and governors of county and voluntary schools. Despite the position of the excepted district between these upper and lower millstones, the Ministry asserted that 'the sum total that can be delegated is far from being a residual assortment of disconnected minor functions . . . the aim is to entrust the council with the day-to-day administration of primary and secondary education in its district and with functions in the field of further education that are essentially local in character'.[2] The medical and dental examination of school children is among the functions which can be delegated.

The Town and Country Planning Act, 1947, following the Education Act, permitted the delegation of planning control functions by county councils to district councils. Regulations made by the Minister in 1964[3] reproduced the concept of county districts with a population of 60,000 or more becoming

---

[1] Such as teachers and caretakers in voluntary aided schools, and any full-time officers of the district council who may, by agreement, be employed part-time on delegated functions.

[2] Ministry of Education Circular 344, December 17, 1958. See also National Association of Divisional Executives for Education *Review*, July 1964.

[3] These replaced Earlier Regulations made in 1959.

excepted councils and being entitled to exercise delegated functions. In special circumstances the Minister of Housing and Local Government may also authorize delegation to a smaller district council which desires to exercise planning control functions.

A somewhat different version of the same theme is found in the National Health Service Act, 1946, which permits area sub-committees to be set up in different parts of a county and authorizes the Health Committee to delegate functions to them.

The next step from these arrangements in regard to individual services, however important, was a leap in the direction of treating delegation as almost the normal means of authorizing county district councils to perform the major part of their functions. In 1957 the Conservative Government issued a White Paper entitled *Functions of County and District Councils in England and Wales*. This contained a reasoned statement on the distribution of powers between county councils and district councils. Its aim was to increase the responsibilities of the district councils, whose powers had been so severely curtailed in the recent past. The district council is local government at a very local level and is assumed to be in closer touch with the people than larger authorities. At the same time it is not always easy to reconcile a transfer of functions to the district level with the needs of efficient administration, especially in the case of services requiring highly qualified specialist staff or a substantial population.[1]

The concordat resulting from negotiations between the local authority associations had agreed that district councils should be entrusted with some functions hitherto exercised by county councils. But no agreement had been reached as to the extent or character of such changes.[2] The White Paper tried to fill in the details by prescribing a population of 60,000 as the minimum figure permitting a district to administer many services then operated by the counties. Thus, nearly all health and welfare functions would be delegated as of right to boroughs and urban districts of 60,000 or more. Delegation to smaller units would occur only in special circumstances. The 60,000

[1] Cmnd 161/1957. Paras 5–7.   [2] *Ibid.*, Paras 1–4.

population figure would give a similar right to boroughs and urban districts to have education and child employment powers delegated to them, except in regard to such matters as teacher training, university awards, advanced further education, boarding schools and youth employment. Classified roads and bridges on such roads, responsibility for the town map in the planning field, the regulation and licensing of theatres and cinemas, inspection of weights and measures, diseases of animals, control of fertilizers and foodstuffs, food and drugs administration—all these functions would be compulsorily delegated without question to urban districts and boroughs over the 60,000 mark. Those of smaller size would be considered on their merits and take their chance.

Rural districts would encounter greater difficulty in entering the heaven of delegated powers. For however large they may be, they are not regarded as a convenient unit of administration for all services. The Government therefore proposed that rural districts would not be entitled to claim delegation automatically whatever their population might be.[1]

All this makes good sense except the insistence of the Government on retaining the principle of delegation—including compulsory delegation—rather than conferment of powers, which had originally been agreed in the concordat reached by the local authority associations.[2] The explanation given in the White Paper is that the Government believes delegation works satisfactorily in some major services; and that it has the advantage of flexibility, which is useful when conditions vary from county to county. This belief in the satisfactory working of delegation is not shared by many persons and bodies well qualified to express an opinion. The Royal Commission on Local Government in Greater London, for example, declared that 'delegation induces a sense of diminished responsibility, particularly in relation to the levying of a rate'.[3] Although it may be useful and even unavoidable in some areas, it produces inevitable stresses and

[1] Cmnd 161/1957. para 16.
[2] See White Paper on Areas and Status of Local Authorities. Cmd 9831/1956, page 15.
[3] Report Cmd 1164/1960, para 259.

strains, and at best is only a way of papering over the cracks caused by dividing a function between a larger and a smaller authority.[1] They carefully avoided introducing delegation into the scheme they propounded for Greater London.

The Local Government Act, 1958, which enacted some but not all of the proposals in the White Paper, authorizes the delegation of numerous health and welfare functions from county councils to county district councils. The functions relate to such matters as the care of mothers and young children, midwives, health visiting, home nursing, vaccination and immunization, the care and after-care of sick persons, the provision of home helps, welfare arrangements for the handicapped, the emergency admission to hospital of mentally ill persons, domiciliary and visiting services to the mentally subnormal, and the registration of private day nurseries and child minders. Certain other functions relating to residential accommodation may be delegated with the consent of the Minister of Health if he is satisfied there are exceptional circumstances to justify so doing.[2] A borough or urban district with a population of 60,000 or more is entitled to a delegation scheme. A smaller county district (whether urban or rural) may have one if the Minister of Health considers that there are special circumstances which make it desirable. Some thirty county district councils have had health and welfare functions delegated to them under these provisions. The Weights and Measures Act, 1963 authorizes delegation to county district councils on the same basis as the Local Government Act, 1958.

Dr Richards, who has made the most extensive study so far published, remarks that in considering whether delegation is worth while it is necessary to know what are its financial consequences, but these are impossible to isolate.[3] He concludes, however, that it clearly makes local administration more complicated and more expensive, but if it increases public interest and participation in government—note the conditional *if*—it may be thought worth while.[4] One of the strangest features of

[1] Report Cmd 1164/1960, para 264.

[2] The Minister has given his consent in only two instances, namely Rhondda and Luton (before the latter had become a county borough).

[3] Peter G. Richards: *Delegation in Local Government*, p. 157.

[4] *Ibid.*, p. 161.

the situation is that delegation has been established by successive governments as the normal method of distributing functions between county and county district councils without any investigation having been carried out as to how it works in practice. Yet it is known to be disliked by many county district councils, and the manner in which it operates varies greatly in different counties. Government Departments have no doubt relied on delegation as a means of mitigating some of the defects of the present local government structure, since it can sidetrack some of the great disparities in the size and resources of county districts.[1]

Some counties regard district councils to which powers have been delegated as mere agents with almost no discretion. Even in its most favourable and liberal-minded manifestations, delegation is a poor substitute for independence and responsibility. Its extensive use indicates a fundamental departure from the British tradition of local government. It has reduced pride, interest and enthusiasm for local government in the boroughs, urban and rural districts.

[1] Report of Royal Commision on Local Government in Greater London, para 256.

VIII

REGIONAL PLANNING

Control over the location of industry was first accepted as a government function in the White Paper on Employment Policy issued in 1944. Machinery was set up by the Board of Trade in Whitehall and in the regions to guide industrialists in the choice of sites for new factories. Regional Boards for Industry were appointed to advise Ministers and their Departments on industrial conditions within their regions and on methods of making fuller use of regional resources. The Boards were intended to inform local industry of government policy and to inform Whitehall of the views held in the regions on industrial questions.

The Boards were composed of representatives of employers and trade unions, and the senior regional officials of a number of interested Departments. There were no members representing local authorities, although the Boards dealt with many questions concerning their work, such as town and country planning, water supplies for industry, day nurseries for employed mothers, housing for key workers, etc.

A more significant by-passing of local authorities occurred with the creation of economic planning councils which the Secretary of State for Economic Affairs (Mr George Brown) set up in 1964 to carry through the ambitious aims of the Labour Government for economic growth. England has been divided into eight great regions, and in each of them there is a Regional Economic Planning Council composed of people with various types of experience and knowledge of the region. Similar Councils have been set up in Scotland and in Wales. The Council assists in the formulation of regional plans and advises on their realization. There is also an executive body known as the Regional Economic Planning Board, composed of civil servants representing the main Government Departments in

41

the region. The chairman is an official of the Department of Economic Affairs.

The Regional Economic Planning Councils have replaced the Regional Boards for Industry. They are expected to have a much more dynamic attitude towards developing the infrastructure and the industry of the region. They will take account of roads and transport, housing, population, schools, hospitals, social services, industrial and commercial location, the labour supply, training facilities, and many other factors of importance to the development of the region. Their terms of reference are: (1) to help in the formulation of a regional plan, having regard to the best use of the region's resources; (2) to advise on the steps necessary for implementing the regional plan on the basis of information and assessment provided by the Economic Planning Board; (3) to advise on the regional implications of national economic policies.

Local authorities as such are not represented on the new Regional Economic Planning Councils. Mr George Brown, the Secretary of State for Economic Affairs, stated in Parliament that he proposed to discuss the procedure for the selection of council members with the local authority associations and other organizations; but he was careful to explain that the members would be appointed in their personal capacity as individuals and not as delegates or representatives of particular interests. In consequence, while local councillors or aldermen may be appointed, they will not sit as representatives of local government.[1]

Executive powers will in any event rest not in the Councils but in the Economic Planning Boards set up in each of the regions to co-ordinate the work on the many Government

---

[1] At a meeting between the First Secretary and local authority associations, to discuss the procedure for securing nominations to the Regional Economic Planning Councils, the Minister indicated that each council would consist of 15–25 members, of whom about a third would come from local authorities in the region. The associations were asked to put forward lists of names from which the Minister could select the persons he desired to appoint. Those on the lists need not necessarily be elected members.

An important point is that the proceedings of the Councils will be confidential; so members who disagree with the advice which is given will not be free to oppose the policy in public. A report of the meeting is printed in the Supplement to the *Municipal Review* for June, 1965, page 117.

Departments concerned with economic development. These boards consist of civil servants, and their creation, according to Mr Brown, 'will not affect the existing powers and responsibilities of local authorities or existing ministerial responsibilities'.[1]

It is obvious that although the new regional organs are supposed to be concerned with economic planning, their work will extend over a far wider field than the purely economic and will affect the activities of local authorities in many different ways. Shortly after Mr Brown had outlined the Government's proposals, *The Times* published a first leader on the subject entitled 'Exit the Town Hall?'[2] The article pointed out that the planning boards come nearer to the French prefecture, and the Regional Advisory Councils are nearer to nominated commissions or corporate bodies, or organs appointed by a process of secret consultation, than either the Boards or the Councils come to the established system of elected local government.

'Local Government', continued *The Times* editorial, 'is a legacy of nineteenth-century interest in democratic forms. It is beginning to look as if confidence in it and practice of it may prove to be a passing phase in British political evolution. The fact that the Government proposes important new departures in regional administration with only a ritual bow to elected representative institutions suggests that there may be a gradual reversion to older forms when the shires were administered by agents of the Crown.'

The 'ritual bow' consisted of the usual assurances by the Department of Economic Affairs that 'the new bodies will not, of course, usurp the functions of the local authorities in the region. They will work in close collaboration with them, and the planning councils will include members with local government experience'[3]—a meaningless phrase. This was a far more negative statement than had appeared in the White Paper on the North East issued by the Conservative Government in 1963. The machinery established at that time also excluded local

---

[1] Parl. Deb. House of Commons Vol. 703. No. 31. December 10, 1964, Cols 1829–1838.

[2] *The Times* newspaper, November 10, 1964.

[3] D.E.A. Progress Report. No. 1. January 1965.

authority representation, but the White Paper declared that 'the part played by local government will of course be vital. Councils will have still more to plan and to do; they will need more staff; and they will also need to co-operate even more than at present with each other. The stronger regional organization of central government will be there to help.'[1] A similar exhortatory statement appeared in the White Paper on Central Scotland issued at the same time.[2]

The Association of Municipal Corporations expressed concern lest the Regional Economic Planning Councils should be unable to exercise an effective check on the planning boards, and deplored the small extent of local government participation. They said that local authorities should have sufficient representation to command the confidence of authorities in the region—whatever that may mean—but they do not want the Regional Councils to have executive responsibility for local government functions, or in any way to displace local government. The Association of Municipal Corporations concedes, however, that it is the Government's right to provide broad overall control of the national economy and also to guide some selected local government functions. Finally, the Association of Municipal Corporations observed that if the Councils are successful the proposal to make them regional elective bodies may arise. The Association thinks they are too large for such a change and that the electorate would be too remote. In their opinion local government in broadly its present form but strengthened by a modicum of reform through the Local Government Commission can meet changing needs.[3]

The Association of Municipal Corporations, like the other local authority organizations, is hamstrung by its own previous utterances resulting from a narrow view of local government based on the interests of municipal corporations. In March 1961 its official organ *The Municipal Review* declared editorially that regionalisation is not local government because it is too far removed from the public. This should not, however, 'make us

---

[1] White Paper on the North East. Cmnd 2206/1963, para 131.
[2] White Paper on Central Scotland. Cmnd 2188/1963, para 161.
[3] A.M.C. Report on Reorganization of Local Government, December 1964, paras 20–21. Approved by General Purposes Committee.

unwilling to face the problem of the need for larger areas in the planning of services, and afraid to try to find a solution compatible with the local nature of true local government'.[1]

The Association of Municipal Corporations had, however, left it at that and done nothing whatever except to recommend the use of joint committees to project local government on to a larger scale. The Association, therefore, could only flutter its wings helplessly in face of the threat to local government posed by the new organs for regional planning and development. Local government, urged the AMC's *Municipal Review*,[2] must firmly insist—by what means was not explained—that none of its powers should be assumed by either the Regional Advisory Councils or the Regional Planning Boards. What a vain hope!

The position taken up by the County Councils Association was even more shortsighted. In May 1964, the Association declared that any approach to local government reform must have as its prime objective the maintenance of the democratic control of local services. The view expressed by Sir Keith Joseph, the Conservative Minister of Housing and Local Government, that regional planning and development must not mean a regional alternative to re-organized local government was in their opinion 'heartening'.[3] By January 1965 the Association resolved 'that the statement [by Mr Brown] be received and that the assurance that the creation of regional planning boards will not affect the existing powers and responsibilities be noted'. This was scarcely an enthusiastic response. The official organ of the County Councils Association expressed the true feelings of the Association in an editorial article acknowledging that 'those who have at heart the values of democracy and independence in local government will surely be keeping an anxious eye on the way things develop over the next few months, lest in their desire to co-ordinate economic planning at regional level the Government allow these values to be eroded away'.[4]

[1] *The Muncipal Review*, March 1961, p. 141.
[2] *Ibid.*, January 1965, pp. 7–10.
[3] *County Councils Association Gazette*, May 1964, p. 103.
[4] *Ibid.*, January 1965. Supplement, p. 31.

Both the Association of Municipal Corporations and the County Councils Association were in a most unhappy position as a result of their own past attitudes. Having for several decades opposed all efforts to introduce a regional element into the local government system, they were now confronted with the only possible alternative: namely, non-elective central government regionalism. In the face of this inevitable nemesis they could do little but wring their hands and express pious hopes about maintaining the values of democracy and independence inherent in local government. For too long have the associations turned not only a blind eye to the writing on the wall, but a deaf ear to the utterances of political scientists who have been warning them about the need for a regional approach to the planning and administration of a number of services.

IX

INCREASED CENTRAL CONTROL

The centralizing tendency which is undermining local government assumes several forms. One form is the straightforward transfer of functions from local authorities to Government Departments or similar organs. This has occurred in regard to trunk roads, hospitals, public assistance, and the valuation of property for rating. A second form consists of the transfer of services and undertakings to *ad hoc* bodies subject to varying degrees of central control. This has happened in the case of the licensing of passenger road services, gas and electricity supply, and other public utility services. Yet another form consists of increased central control over local authorities. There are many manifestations of this.

The introduction of the Block Grant in 1929 was accompanied by a provision which for the first time gave the Minister of Health power to reduce the grants by any amount he thought fit, if he considered that the expenditure of a council had been excessive, having regard to its financial resources and other relevant circumstances.[1] The same enactment gave Whitehall vast new powers over the whole field of public health and highway administration, for the Minister was authorized to reduce the grant by whatever amount he thought fit if he were satisfied that a local authority had 'failed to achieve or maintain a reasonable standard of efficiency and progress in the discharge of their functions relating to public health services', regard being had to the standard maintained in other areas, or if the Minister of Transport certified that a council had failed to maintain their roads, or any part of them, in a satisfactory condition.

These powers have been enlarged in successive Acts which have followed and replaced the original legislation. The latest

[1] Local Government Act, 1929, Section 104.

statement is to be found in the Local Government Act, 1958, which introduced the General Grant. This provides that if the appropriate Minister is satisfied that a recipient authority has failed to achieve or maintain reasonable standards in the provision of any of the services giving rise to relevant expenditure, regard being had to the standards maintained in other areas, he can (with the approval of the House of Commons) reduce the General Grant by any amount he thinks fit.

The services in respect of which Ministers can exercise these powers include education, the functions of local health authorities in connection with the national health service, fire brigades, town and country planning, services under the Children Act, services relating to road safety, the enforcement of the law affecting road traffic, the provision of facilities for physical training and recreation, and the provision of accommodation under the National Assistance Act.[1] Not a word of protest was uttered by local councils or their associations at the acquisition by the central government of these vast new powers.

The General Grant gives more apparent freedom to local authorities in the exercise of discretion regarding the scale and standard of their services than existed under the percentage grants for particular services which it replaced. In consequence, the detailed controls by central Departments have been somewhat eased. But as the General Grant is based on the average expenditure of local authorities on various services, it can work in the opposite direction and have a restrictive effect on the freedom of local authorities. As Sir William Hart points out, they may be deterred from taking bold decisions which, if centrally approved, could formerly have been taken 'in the conforting knowledge that percentage grants would automatically have matched the expenditure locally incurred. In the changed circumstances of today, when grant income exceeds the income drawn from the rates, real scope for choice might in fact prove wider under the theoretically more restricted percentage grant than under the block grant.'[2]

The erosion of local independence and freedom is not a new

[1] Local Government Act, 1958, 1st Schedule, parts I and II.
[2] Sir William Hart: 'The Structure of Local Government' in *Local Government Today and Tomorrow*. Ed. Dudley Lofts, p. 25.

phenomenon. In the so-called financial crisis of 1931 the central government exercised a dominating influence of an unprecedented kind over local authorities. In the course of the panic measures which were taken by the Government to reduce public expenditure at the very time when it should have been increased, the then Chancellor of the Exchequer instructed the associations of local authorities that in order to 'lighten the heavy burden at present borne by the community' they were to review the whole field of local expenditure in order to effect reductions at the earliest possible moment. At the same time the Minister of Health (who was then in general charge of local government) using language without precedent in the history of his Department, announced in a circular that as regards salary reductions His Majesty's Government did not think it practicable to impose any hard-and-fast rule on local authorities. 'Impose' was a new word for the central government to employ towards the ancient counties and proud cities of Britain. Yet it was one to which they were soon to become accustomed, for the National Economy Act, 1931, enabled the Government to make Orders in Council for the purpose of effecting economies in regard to education, police, roads, etc., and also 'for imposing duties on local authorities in connection with the administration of any such service'. Neither resentment nor resistance appear to have been aroused by this successful attempt by the central government to dominate local authorities.

Yet the significance of what had occurred was unmistakable. 'It is indisputable', I wrote at the time, that these events 'betoken a subordination of local autonomy to the dictates of the central power which, if pursued, will be the virtual end of local government. The complete abdication by the local authorities of the right to think and act for themselves; their transformation into mere receptacles for Government policy; their immediate acceptance of all the ill-considered panic measures, involving a complete reversal of existing tendencies and the abrogation of carefully-prepared schemes, put forward by the Government under the pretext of the so-called crisis; their servile acquiescence without a protest in the unlimited encroachment on the rights of local authorities introduced by the National Economy Act, 1931; their willingness to destroy and to see destroyed the fruits of municipal progress in terms of education, housing, and the other social services without so much as an enquiry into the necessity for so doing—all this, I suggest, reveals a new and degraded spirit in local government which has not previously appeared in this country.'[1]

It would be quite wrong to assume that the tendency towards centralization has occurred only in times of financial emergency or war. The long term trends point in the same direction.

The Education Act, 1944, for example, declared that it is the duty of the Minister of Education [and Science] *inter alia* 'to secure the effective execution by local authorities, under his control and direction, of the national policy for providing a varied and comprehensive educational service in every area'. Here again we confront a new relationship between central government and local authorities. Hitherto that relation had been largely a partnership, with the exception of the former Poor Law, which never recovered from the absolute subordination of local authorities to the central power laid down in the Poor Law Act, 1834.[2] In the field of education the idea of a partnership had been specially prevalent. Throughout the whole range of functions which Parliament has assigned to local government the principle has prevailed that local authorities derive their powers from the law and are free to exercise them within the limits laid down by legislation or regulations made under statutory authority, subject to such limited degree of ministerial direction or approval as may be specified and to the supervisory jurisdiction of the Courts. The Education Act, 1944, broke new ground by conferring on the Minister of Education [and Science] power to prevent the unreasonable exercise of their functions by education authorities. If, says the Act,[3] the Minister is satisfied, either on complaint by any person or otherwise, that any local education authority or the managers or governors of any county or voluntary school have acted or are proposing to act unreasonably with respect to the

---

[1] 'The Central Domination of Local Government', by W. A. Robson, 4, *Political Quarterly*, January–March 1933, p. 89.

[2] It is significant that the Education Act, 1944, used the same language, 'control and direction' to describe the relationship between the central department and the local authorities as the Poor Law.   [3] Section 68.

exercise of any power conferred or the performance of any duty imposed upon them, he may give them such directions as to the exercise of the power or the performance of the duty as he thinks expedient. This over-riding provision applies even where the law expressly states that the duty or power is contingent upon the opinion of the local education authority or school managers or governors. The Minister need not wait for a complaint in order to act. He can intervene on his own initiative at any time.

Thus the local education authority is no longer regarded as competent to judge what is a reasonable use of their discretionary powers. Parliament confers powers on local authorities and the Courts are available to see that they are not exceeded or abused. But henceforth the Minister is deemed to be the final repository of reason and his decision cannot be challenged either in the Courts or directly in Parliament. His opinion, moreover, is placed above the views of the local electors. This far-reaching and absolute control is bound to permeate and influence the relationship between the Ministry of Education and local education authorities in regard to every matter, great or small, which concerns the latter's work.[1]

We shall no doubt be told by apologists for the type of central domination which is now emerging that this provision will be seldom, if ever, used. The late Montagu Harris excused on precisely this ground the sweeping powers of the Minister of Health to reduce the Block Grant which have been mentioned above. 'Even so far as this provision does reserve to the Minister a power of financial control,' he wrote, 'it would seem probable that, as in all such cases, such power will be seldom exercised. It may be held over the local authorities as a threat, and, for the very reason that it is so much wider than the previous power of withholding specific percentage grants, it is perhaps even less likely to be put into force.'[2] Therefore, he argued, we must not assume that the Minister will frequently depart from the usual procedure of persuasion.

To regard the matter from this angle is completely mis-

---

[1] See 'Ministry Control and Local Autonomy in Education', by John A. Brand, 36 *Political Quarterly*, p. 154.

[2] G. Montagu Harris: *Muncipal Self-Government in Britain*, pp. 208–9.

leading. In England it is seldom necessary for administrative authorities to invoke their legal powers when dealing with one another. Matters are discussed in a gentlemanly and urbane manner, with the stronger party often being the first to suggest a compromise in the gentlest manner. But everyone knows where the whip hand lies—and acts accordingly. There are, Sir Ivor Jennings rightly said, consequences of this close control which are psychological in character and hence outside the ambit of any statutory enactment.[1] The present Minister of Education and Science still uses the language of partnership in dealing with local education authorities, and this will no doubt continue as a matter of form. 'But that is not the language of the Act', the Mayor of Lincoln complained, 'with its reference to control and direction. It is the language of principal and agent.'[2]

[1] W. Ivor Jennings: *Principles of Local Government Law*, 2nd ed., p. 245.

[2] Alderman J. W. F. Hill: See Report of Proceedings at Conference on Local Government of Association of Municipal Corporations, September 25 and 26, 1946, p. 37.

X

LOCAL DEPENDENCE ON CENTRAL FINANCE

The growth of central control here depicted must include some mention of the increasing part played by Exchequer grants in local government finance. The broad outlines of the position are shown in Table I on page 54:

From this Table it can be seen that until 1950–51 local authorities received more from rates than from grants.[1] In 1950–51 the sums received from these two sources were approximately equal. Since then, the sums received from central grants have been growing both as regards the total amount and in proportion to the money yielded by the rates. In 1933 the ratio of grants to rates was 5 : 6. In 1964 the ratio was 5 : 4½.[2] Local authorities spent in 1964 on revenue account over £2,700m a year or about one-eleventh of the national income. Of this only about a third came from the rates.

The very large increase both in the absolute amount of grants and in the proportion which they bear to rate revenue is both a cause and a consequence of an increase of central control. The diminished independence of local authorities is a reflection of, and is in turn reflected by, the diminished role of local sources of revenue. Can anyone seriously doubt that as the Treasury comes to provide more and more money for the local councils, the voices of Whitehall will speak more often and with greater insistence?

The present position has not come about by inadvertence.

[1] During the Second World War special subventions were given in respect of Civil Defence and other emergency services which have been disregarded owing to their abnormal character.

[2] I am not, however, arguing that the increasing subservience of local authorities to Whitehall is wholly due to their dependence on grants. It has been accurately remarked that there is 'a vast apparatus of detailed central control of local affairs . . . which has nothing to do with the form of Exchequer grants'. D. S. Lees: *Local Expenditure and Exchequer Grants*, p. 167 (1956).

TABLE I: LOCAL GOVERNMENT INCOME
REVENUE ACCOUNT ($£m$)

Year	Rates	% from Rates	Grants	% from Grants	Miscel-laneous	% from Misc.	% of Grants to Rates
1933–34	148·6	33·3	121·6	27·2	176·4	39·5	82
1938–39	191·4	35·2	140·2	25·8	212·3	39·0	73
1947–48	283·3	29·4	269·7	28·0	410·2	42·6	95
1950–51	304·9	33·9	304·6	33·9	289·8	32·2	100
1953–54	392·5	33·4	414·2	35·2	369·6	31·4	106
1956–57	513·5	33·0	568·0	36·5	474·2	30·5	111
1959–60	649·9	33·3	705·6	36·2	593·5	30·5	109
1961–62	747·4	33·0	830·6	36·7	690·2	30·4	111
1962–63	831·3	33·4	907·0	36·4	753·6	30·2	109
1963–64	923·1	33·3	1022·4	36·9	826·7	29·8	111

(The column headed 'Miscellaneous' is made up of receipts from rents, charges, fees, income from trading services etc. The figures are taken from Local Government Financial Statistics 1962–63, Table X and later estimates.)

Local government finance has been under almost continuous examination and discussion during the past ten years—and is still being inquired into by central departments, local authorities and their associations. Hitherto, those august bodies have shown a masterly ability to overlook or to avoid the really important questions and to get bogged down in the meticulous discussion of minor issues.

In 1957, following what Mr Brooke, the then Minister of Housing and Local Government, called a thorough review of the subject, a White Paper on Local Government Finance was published.[1] Simultaneously with the Government review, a major research study had been undertaken by the Royal Institute of Public Administration which was published under the title *New Sources of Local Revenue*; and another by the Institute of Municipal Treasurers and Accountants into Local Expenditure and Exchequer Grants. The results of these two research projects by highly competent professional organizations were made available to the Government before publication. The White Paper made a passing reference to this 'valuable research'—and then with superb complacency ignored both studies completely.

The Conservative Government's main conclusions were announced early in 1957, before publication of the White Paper. The most important decisions were a flat rejection of any alternative or additional source of local taxation for local authorities; a refusal to authorize the collection of a local income tax; and a refusal to earmark for local authorities, or to hand over to them, in whole or part, any of the taxes levied by the central government, such as those on motor spirit or entertainments. In the Government's view 'improvement of the system of local finance must come from improvements of the system of local taxation which is traditionally the right of local authorities, combined with a radical recasting of the system of grants'.[2]

Mr Brooke declared that rates are considered to be a sound basis for local finance; that no better system of local taxation

---

[1] Cmnd. 209/1957. H.M.S.O.
[2] Parl. Debates. House of Commons, Vol. 564, Cols. 1077–1085 (February 12, 1957); White Paper on Local Government Finance, paras 7–12, 13–34.

has been propounded; and that it was 'impracticable'—for reasons which he did not explain—to allow local authorities to have any new source of income within their own control. The Government's main proposals were to re-rate from 25 to 50 per cent industrial and freight-transport heraditaments; to replace most of the percentage grants by a General Grant; and to revise the system of Equalisation Grants.[1] The ostensible reason for abolishing the percentage grant system was that it entailed the danger of excessive central supervision and left the Exchequer without precise knowledge of its future liabilities. Emphasis was also laid on the desire to give greater independence to local authorities in the raising and spending of their money in order to improve the health of local government.[2]

By far the greatest need in the sphere of finance is to make local authorities less dependent than they are at present on grants from the Exchequer. Legally there is no limit to the amount which they can raise by means of the rates. In practice there are very severe limitations arising from the regressive nature of this particular tax, and the psychological resistance and political opposition of ratepayers to rates which approach or exceed 20s. in the £.

The much vaunted freedom of local authorities in regard to the rates is greatly exaggerated. Intervention by the central government in the rating system has occurred frequently. The Government of the day derated industrial and freight-transport premises in 1929 to 25 per cent of their annual value, re-rated them to 50 per cent in 1958 and to 100 per cent in 1963. Agricultural land has for long been entirely freed of rating liability. Revaluation of all types of premises was held up by successive legislative enactments from 1939 until 1957, so that only a small proportion of their true value was taken as a basis for calculating rates. The Rating and Valuation Act, 1957, enacted that shops, offices and other commercial properties should be rated at only 80 per cent of their annual value,[3] largely in order to protect the Government from the wide-

[1] Parl. Debates. House of Commons, Vol. 564, Cols. 1077–1085 (February 12, 1957); White Paper on Local Government Finance, paras. 7–12, 13–34.

[2] White Paper, para. 5, Parl. Debates, House of Commons, Vol. 654 (February 12, 1957), Col. 1078.

[3] S. 1. If part is used for a private dwelling the figure was raised to 86 per cent.

spread resentment of shopkeepers and office occupiers at the revaluation for rating purposes introduced in that year. The derating of premises used by charities is another matter on which the central government has laid down policy, although a greater measure of discretion is now given to the rating authorities.[1] The quinquennial rating revaluation due in 1968 has been abandoned by the Government because of the pressure of work imposed on the Inland Revenue's Valuation Office by the creation of the Land Commission.

Despite the tribute to the rating system paid by Mr Brooke as Minister of Housing and Local Government, the Conservative Government's awareness of its defects was shown in several ways. The White Paper on Local Government Finance propounded a new Rate Deficiency Grant (to replace the Equalization Grants introduced in 1948). The Rate Deficiency Grant is payable to local authorities in areas where the product of a penny rate is less than the average or standard product of a penny rate for that area. This is calculated as a proportion based on population of the national average yield of a penny rate.[2] The Rate Deficiency Grant makes the Exchequer in effect an additional ratepayer, responsible for about 14 per cent of the rates of the entire country.

The need for Rate Deficiency Grants arises from the fact that about 300 wealthy local authorities situated in Greater London, the Home Counties, the larger seaside resorts and some of the regional capitals have less than a third of the national population but possess nearly half of the rateable value of the country. As a result, the great majority of local authorities, in whose areas two-thirds of the population lives, have a rateable capacity per head below the national average. It is among these local authorities, numbering about 1,227 in 1963–64, that the Rate Deficiency Grant was distributed to the extent of about £152m a year.[3]

Another drawback of the rates was implied by the appoint-

[1] Rating and Valuation Act, 1961. S. 11.
[2] Local Government Act, 1958. S. 5. A weighting factor for sparsity of population is added.
[3] The Working of the Rate Deficiency Grants in England and Wales. Report of the Working Party (1962), paras 5, 8; Report of the Allen Committee of Inquiry into the Impact of Rates on Households. Cmnd. 2582/1965, paras 27–28.

ment of the Allen Committee to assess the impact of rates on households in different income groups and in different parts of Great Britian, with special regard to any circumstances likely to give rise to hardship. When the appointment of this Committee was announced in May 1963, the Minister stated there would be no standstill or any relief in hardship cases until the Committee had reported, after which the Government would decide if anything needed to be done.[1] Nevertheless, before the Allen Committee had reported, the Government had climbed down and introduced the Rating (Interim Relief) Act, 1964, which enabled rating authorities in areas where there had been a steep rise in the rates of not less than a quarter to relieve residential occupiers of part of the increase by means of a remission or refund. The Minister was required to pay a grant to the rating authority equal to slightly more than half the amount given or forgone by way of relief.[2] In addition, a per capita grant of £5 was payable to rating authorities having an abnormally high proportion of persons over 65 years of age in their areas. This money was in aid of their revenue generally.[3]

The Act of 1964, as its title indicates, was only a temporary expedient pending the report of the Allen Committee. Another expedient was contained in the Rating Bill introduced by Mr Crossman in December 1965. This provides for rate rebates to be allowed to occupiers of small means. The maximum rebate, amounting to two thirds of the rates in excess of £7 10s. will be given to a single person (whether unmarried, separated or widowed) if his or her income is not more than £416 a year or £8 a week. The full rebate will by £8 on rates of £20, £22 on rates of £40, or £35 on rates of £60. A married couple will be entitled to the full rebate if their joint income is not more than £520 a year or £10 a week. If there are children in the household the maximum income is raised. Where the ratepayer's income exceeds the specified maximum, the amount of the rebate is reduced by 5s. for every pound above the limit.

This complex scheme aims at easing the burden of rates

[1] Parl. Deb. House of Commons, Vol. 677, Col. 642, May 9, 1963.
[2] Rating (Interim Relief) Act, 1964.
[3] For a Survey on the working of the Act, See *Rating and Valuation*, August–September 1964.

falling on about two million occupiers. It involves a means test which will be carried out by the finance staffs of the rating authorities. Three quarters of the cost will be borne by the Exchequer and the remainder by the other ratepayers in each area.

This elaborate measure, like the Rating (Interim Relief) Act, 1964, is intended to be only a temporary expedient pending a fundamental revision of the system of local taxation. It is an Act to relieve the poorer householders rather than to assist local authorities. Indeed, by imposing a new and unwelcome task on municipal officers, of conducting a means test by increasing yet further the ratio of grants to rates, and by demonstrating once again how far-reaching is central control over rating policy, the new Bill is detrimental to the interests of local government.

Mr Crossman, in introducing the Bill, made the most forthright denunciation of the rating system ever made by a Minister responsible for local government. He attacked the rates first on the ground of the 'intrinsic iniquities' in the method of arriving at rateable values, and second on account of their regressive character. These defects, he declared, are so vicious that they cannot be removed by revaluation. They are 'undermining the strength of local government and enforcing a slow takeover by central government. The more you are forced to shift the burden from the shoulders of the ratepayer to those of the taxpayer, the more you strengthen Whitehall against the town hall.'[1] He wished to see the ultimate abolition of rating, and its replacement by a new local tax which would be fair, intelligible, and capable of being efficiently administered.

What the Minister had in mind has not yet been revealed. A week later he stated in answer to a question in Parliament that a fairer method of local taxation must depend on the future structure of local government and that he would have no specific proposals for such a tax for some time to come.[2] In an interview with the Editor of *The Local Government Chronicle*[3]

[1] Parl. Debates. House of Commons, Vol. 722, Cols. 40, 41 (December 6, 1965).
[2] Parl. Debates. House of Commons, Vol. 722. Written Answers, Col. 229 (December 14, 1965)
[3] September 25, 1965, p. 1476.

Mr Crossman was reported as saying that he had reluctantly come to the conclusion that there was no substitute for rating nor any tax which could be used as a substitute.

It is an undoubted gain that the Minister of Housing and Local Government should perceive as clearly as Mr Crossman does the serious defects of the present system of local taxation and the disastrous consequences of an ever-increasing reliance by local authorities on central grants. It is unlikely that he or any other Minister will be able to find an entirely new method of taxation to replace the rates, for in most countries local authorities derive most of their revenue from taxes on real property. While there are many other sources of taxation which could and should be used to supplement revenue from rates, it is difficult to think of any which could wholly replace it. A local income tax is most unlikely to be adopted by any British Government within the foreseeable future in view of the extremely heavy burden of direct taxation already levied on earned and unearned income.

During the past year Mr Crossman hinted that one possible alternative souce of local revenue might be a share of motor vehicle duties which local authorities collect for the central government'.[1] This would certainly be only a supplementary source of income for local authorities. Another straw in the wind is that a considerable number of local councillors and Labour Party supporters urge that the whole cost of education, or at least the cost of teachers' salaries, should be borne by the Exchequer. This would merely exacerbate all the evil tendencies in the present situation. If it were to happen it would no longer be possible to claim that education is a local government service in any meaningful sense of the term. Mr Crossman, speaking in July 1965 at Hove, said that the Government were pledged to give early relief to ratepayers by transferring the larger part of public expenditure from local authorities to the Exchequer. This policy will be in complete disregard of the warning he gave in the House of Commons of the consequences to local government of shifting the burden from the ratepayer to the taxpayer.

It is abundantly clear, however, that the rating system is not

[1] See *The Times*, June 14, 1965, p. 6, for a report of his talk on television.

by itself an adequate or satisfactory source of local taxation It is inadequate in terms of its potential yield; inequitable as between rating areas; and regressive in its incidence. It has to be bolstered by a large Rate Deficiency Grant, which adds to the dependence of local authorities for their income on the Exchequer. The fact that a Working Party on Rate Deficiency Grants reported that in their opinion 'the system finds general acceptance'[1] means little except that local authorities and their associations are short-sighted enough to find acceptable almost any device by which grants are poured into their ever-open mouths.

I have already described the far reaching powers acquired by Ministers for influencing or controlling local authorities by reducing (or threatening to reduce) the General Grant if any one or more of a long list of services is not provided at a reasonable standard, having regard to what other authorities do. This is presumably intended to impose a national minimum standard. The Rate Deficiency Grant is calculated on a new formula, the effect of which is to limit the amount of the Grant payable to any one authority by reference to the 'normal' expenditure of other authorities of the same class. The 'normal' expenditure is simply the average amount spent per head during the preceding three years by the group of local authorities concerned. Thus, an urban district council's 'normal' expenditure is based on the average expenditure per head of all urban districts. A council which spends substantially more than the average of its class will usually be left to pay for its own excess expenditure. The effect of these provisions is to induce local authorities to follow the average line of conduct; to pursue mediocrity at all costs lest a fate worse than death await them in the shape of reduced exchequer grants.

The White Paper on Local Government Finance stated that while the Government must still remain responsible for laying down national policy and for ensuring compliance with basic standards in grant-aided services, a greater measure of local financial independence was a primary aim of the changes and 'the maximum local discretion will be given in the method of

---

[1] The Working of the Rate Deficiency Grants in England and Wales. Report of The Working Party (1962), paras 9 and 10.

providing the service'.[1] One may accept the need for the central government to lay down the general lines of policy which local authorities are required to follow and to see that they observe a national minimum standard in the basic services; but I do not believe that any large degree of freedom is likely to be given to local authorities in the spending of money unless they are given access to new and additional sources of local taxation entirely within their own control. Exchequer grants will always have strings attached to them, whatever a White Paper may say, and the reluctance of successive Ministers to broaden the narrow tax base now available to local authorities is probably due to a conscious or unconscious desire to keep them in leading strings. There can scarcely be any rational grounds for not allowing local authorities to have a share of the petrol tax or motor licence duty or the entertainments tax, or to levy a tax on cats or bicycles if they wish, or to impose a retail sales tax.[2]

The General Grant, which replaced percentage grants to the value of £300m a year, is based on the weighted population of the area of each recipient authority, supplemented by grants for specified factors such as the number of children under 5 years, the number of old persons over 65 years, the number of children in council schools, density of population, road mileage in relation to population, etc. The formula is presumable intended to ensure that the grant allows for the principal factors which will influence the expenditure of each local authority. Thereafter, the responsibility of the central government is supposed to be limited to seeing that no local authority fails to achieve a minimum prescribed standard in the provision of services; and it is assumed that a grant based on a formula of this kind calls for much less central inspection and control than percentage grants.

This was the substance of the Minister's repeated assurances during the parliamentary debates on the Local Government Bill which introduced these changes.[3] 'The theme of the financial provisions', said Mr Brooke, 'is to strengthen the local char-

[1] Local Government Finance, Cmnd 209/1957, para. 13.
[2] For a full discussion see New Sources of Local Revenue, Royal Institute of Public Administration (1956).
[3] Parl. Deb. House of Commons, Vol. 579, Col. 902; (December 9, 1957). Ibid., Vol. 564, Col. 1079 (February 12, 1957).

acter of local government through enabling local authorities to exercise greater responsibility over the spending of money in their areas.' The White Paper stated that the local authorities had proposed a fresh review of central controls over local government, and this had been accepted by the Government.[1]

The only result so far of this heart-searching exercise by the Government is the enactment of a provision conferring on local authorities the right to spend a sum equal to the proceeds of a penny rate on anything they choose which is in the interests of the area or its inhabitants.[2] This magnificent act of confidence and generosity on the part of the Ministry of Housing and Local Government opened up at one stroke a dazzling vista of freedom and opportunity for local authorities. One can imagine the sense of release from the long years of bondage, the intoxicating feeling of a new era having dawned, which must have filled the hearts of Councillors and Aldermen, Town Clerks and County Treasurers, as they tried to comprehend the full import of this revolutionary measure. One pictures delegations from great cities and ancient counties returning from Whitehall and Westminster with tears of joy in their eyes as they seemed to hear the noise of 'the free penny' jingling in their pockets. One pictures the firework displays, the barbecue in the market place, the great bonfires, the dancing of the citizens in the streets, the civic receptions, which must have greeted the homecoming of the delegates who achieved this great victory. Even in the parishes, where the prospect of wild extravagance in the pursuit of civic virtue offered by the free penny was reduced to rather less than a farthing (one-fifth of a penny, to be precise), one pictures the Lord of the Manor offering a meat tea to his faithful parishioners, and the local innkeeper providing free drinks to all so long as the supply of beer lasted. Will not the Local Government (Financial Provisions) Act, 1963, take its place eventually beside Magna Carta, the Bill of Rights and other great constitutional documents which mark the milestones on the road to freedom?

The local authority associations seem never to have grasped

---

[1] White Paper on Local Government Finance. Cmnd. 209/1957, para 5.
[2] Local Government (Financial Provisions) Act, 1963. S. 6.

the nature of the financial malaise from which local government has for long been suffering. The Association of Municipal Corporations pointed out in its official organ *The Municipal Review* in January 1954 that the financial resources of local authorities were insufficient to meet the demands made upon them, and added that the re-rating of industrial and freight-transport premises would be a most suitable first step in rectifying the position.[1] A little later they asked for a general grant towards the expenses of all local authorities together with a grant based on need.[2] The Equalization Grant was criticized partly on the ground that twenty-eight county boroughs did not qualify for receipt of the grant,[3] and partly because the valuation basis did not reveal the true extent of need. In 1956 the association made representations to the Chancellor of the Exchequer for an immediate review of local authority finance, the reasons for this demand being the purely adventitious factors of the credit squeeze cuts in the housing susbsidies, and the recent making of new valuation lists.[4] In April 1957 the Association of Municipal Corporations expressed pleasure at the re-rating of industry and welcomed the impending disappearance of the percentage grants.

A little later, in reviewing the White Paper on Local Government Finance, the Association declared that the important feature of the proposed grant was the amount involved. If it were insufficient local authorities would feel they had no room to move and all ideas of greater freedom resulting from it would be stultified. It was for the Government to satisfy local authorities that it was not their intention to strangle incentive and enterprise[5]—and so on in the same vein.

At no point did the Association show the slightest awareness of the importance of keeping the ratio of grants to rates at a lower figure than that which had already been reached. It was on the amount of the new general grant that their attention was riveted, not its relation to locally raised income; and the Association seems never to have put forward a request for new

[1] *Municipal Review*, January 1954, p. 2.   [2] *Ibid.*, November 1954, p. 187.
[3] *Ibid.*, January 1954, p. 187.   [4] *Ibid.*, May 1956, p. 93.
[5] *Ibid.*, September 1957, pp. 375–76.

sources of local revenue. Thus, in May 1960, their official organ declared that 'a proper rateable value for all property is the key to local government finance and also to the continued independence of local government'.[1] Even when re-rating of industry, freight-transport undertakings and shops had been brought about, the Association protested strongly at a reduction in future general grants as a partial off-setting of local authorities' increased revenue from this source.[2]

The other local authority associations have displayed an equally myopic attitude towards financial questions. The County Councils Association declared in 1957 that the general grant 'could hardly fail to enhance the status of local authorities'; it considered that the re-rating of industry was a step in the right direction but disapproved of the Government's intention to reduce Exchequer grants by a corresponding amount.[3]

In 1963 the County Councils Association issued a report which examined the present rating system, the possibilities of assigned revenues, site value rating, a poll tax, a sales tax, a local income tax, and Government Grants. The conclusions at which the Report arrived were: '(a) That the most fruitful field of further study, with the object of increasing the revenue of local authorities, lies in the relationship between government grants and rates; (b) That the difficulties, social, political and economic, involved in the adoption of any of the alternative sources of revenue which have been examined are such as to inhibit, if not entirely preclude, their introduction into our fiscal system.'[4] In a separate report on 'The Relationship between Government Grants and Rates' issued in May 1964, the Association pointed out that whereas local authority expenditure is expected to rise by 74 per cent in the next decade, the gross national product will increase by only 48 per cent. The present level of rates is only just tolerable and could not bear any increase beyond that resulting from the growth of the gross national product. This would leave a sum of £194m

---

[1] *Muncipal Review*, May 1960, p. 301.   [2] *Ibid.*, February 1963, pp. 81–2.
[3] *County Councils Association Gazette*, March 1957, p. 41, see also the Report of the C.C.A. Finance Committee, *C.C.A. Gazette*, July 1957.
[4] *The Rating System and Local Revenue*, para 87.

to be found in 1971–72 and £224m in 1972–73. Rates cannot bear all this without endangering the system. The rest will have to come from the Exchequer.[1]

The only trace of uneasiness displayed by the report of the County Councils Association was that the word 'grant' 'inevitably conveys a feeling among local authorities that their status is fundamentally subservient'; but they dismissed this feeling as 'entirely illusory', for local authorities are as fully entitled to what they receive from grants as to their income from rates. The raising and paying of money by the central government to local authorities is in their eyes no different in essence from the function of local authorities in collecting and paying over to the central government the motor taxation revenue and other national taxes.[2] It would be hard to find a greater capacity for self-deception than this report reveals.

The Urban District Councils Association holds similar views —so similar, indeed, that their sub-committee on Local Government Finance decided that there would be no point in issuing a report which merely reiterated the views expressed by the AMC and the CCA, with which they were in full agreement. The points they stressed were that part of the general grant should be distributed direct to urban district councils, and that the taxpayer should bear a larger share of the cost of education.[3]

The Rural District Councils Association have produced nothing on the subject of finance in recent years. The Association is understood to regard the AMC report on finance with approval and to be satisfied with the working of the General Grant and the Rate Deficiency Grant.

These pronouncements make one despair of any revival of local government. Local authorities seem to be not only subservient to the Central Government but satisfied with their subservience. They are no longer partners in a common enter-

---

[1] Report of Working Party on The Relationship between Government Grants and Rates, para 25.

[2] *Ibid.*, paras 14–17.

[3] Urban District Councils Association. Minutes of Meeting on February 5, 1965, p. 30.

prise but only junior partners[1] or mere administrative agents of the central power.

The passages quoted above are typical of the attitude of local authorities and their associations over the years. They have been obsessed by the desire for ever larger Exchequer Grants, regardless of the growing domination by this source of revenue of their total resources. They have continually demanded more and more money from the central government without thought of the consequences. They have failed to understand the political advantages of enlarging the basis of local taxation.

Very recently, however, the Association of Municipal Corporations has come out with some proposals for improving the rating system and for obtaining additional sources of local revenue.[2] As regards the former, the AMC report advocates the full rating of farm and forestry land, and recommends as a first step the immediate rerating of buildings used for producing, by modern industrial methods, eggs, poultry, livestock, flowers, tomatoes and vegetables. The owners of empty property should be required to pay charges for access and protection services provided by local authorities. Charities should pay the full rateable value of their premises, but local authorities should use the discretionary powers they have to help charities. Nationalized industries and public utilities should be liable to pay rates on a realistic basis irrespective of their financial viability.

As regards additional sources of local revenue, the Association of Municipal Corporations has at last begun to look at the various possibilities with a more open mind. They see no merit in examining a local income tax, a poll tax, the retention of motor vehicle licence duties, a local sales tax, a local entertainment tax, a tax on bicycles, or an addition to national insurance contributions. The fiscal ideas they consider to be worth pursuing are a tax on advertising posters; a percentage levy on betting, whether in betting shops, bookmakers or fruit

[1] The statement that 'local government is the junior partner' appeared in the CCA Report on 'The Relationship between Government Grants and Rates', para 24.

[2] *The Reform of Rating.* Report by the Rating Committee of the AMC, November 18, 1965.

machines; a charge on restaurant meals (excluding alcoholic drinks) and hotel accommodation; the taxation of land values or a levy on development rights; and finally the taxing of motor vehicles in proportion to road use, with particular reference to a levy on cars using congested roads.

The AMC report[1] is far too ready to dismiss possible taxes which are known to be practicable from experience in other countries, such as a local sales tax or a local entertainment tax. For example, it rejects a local sales tax in eleven lines on the grounds that 'we do not know that there is any enthusiasm' for such taxes in the countries which have them; that they are confusing to shoppers; and that they are equivalent to the purchase tax, which is a not a popular tax. But who ever heard of a popular tax or one which evoked enthusiasm? The report is also unduly sceptical about what it calls the 'economic viability' of such taxes as a supplementary local levy on petrol sales. But it is at least a pleasant change to see the AMC thinking about something other than increased Exchequer grants.

Mr Crossman or his successor would do well to give immediate attention to these and other suggestions for improving the rating system and providing local authorities with new sources of income, without waiting for some far-distant scheme to abolish the rates altogether and to substitute a better (but at present unknown) method of local taxation.

---

[1] *Supplementary Sources of Local Revenue.* Report by the General Purposes Committee of the AMC, November 18, 1965.

XI

A DIAGNOSIS

The reasons for these drastic symptoms of decline are clear. For more than forty years the organization of local government has been growing obsolete and is now hopelessly out of date.

The local authorities in England and Wales on April 1, 1965 comprised:

58 county councils
82 county borough councils
276 non-county borough councils
548 urban district councils } a total of 1298
474 rural district councils } District Councils
About 7,500 parish councils
About 3,400 parish meetings

The list does not include Greater London, which has the Greater London Council, 32 London Borough Councils and the City Corporation.

If we classify the local authorities according to population, we get the following figures:

TABLE II: POPULATION OF LOCAL AUTHORITIES IN ENGLAND AND WALES (mid-1964)

Population	Number
Above 1,000,000	4 County councils 1 County borough council
500,000 to 1,000,000	14 County councils 3 County borough councils
250,000 to 500,000	15 London Borough councils 17 County councils 10 County borough councils

69

Population	Number
100,000 to 250,000	17 London borough councils 14 County councils 33 County borough councils 1 Non-county borough council 2 Urban district councils 2 Rural district councils
50,000 to 100,000	5 County councils 34 County borough councils 45 Non-county borough councils 17 Urban district councils 27 Rural district councils
20,000 to 50,000	3 County councils 1 County borough council 94 Non-county borough councils 130 Urban district councils 164 Rural district councils
10,000 to 20,000	1 County council 53 Non-county borough councils 162 Urban district councils 160 Rural district councils
5,000 to 10,000	38 Non-county borough councils 129 Urban district councils 82 Rural district councils
1,000 to 5,000	44 Non-county borough councils 104 Urban district councils 39 Rural district councils
Below 1,000	1 Non-county borough council 4 Urban district councils

(Source: Registrar General's Population Estimates for Mid-1964.)

The differences in population among areas of the same constitutional class are almost grotesque. The counties range from Lancashire, with more than two and a quarter million, to Rutland with less than thirty thousand. The West Riding of Yorkshire has 1,696,220 inhabitants, Westmorland only 66,950. The Welsh counties vary from Glamorganshire with more than three-quarters of a million to Radnorshire with less than 20,000. Even if we omit the extremes there are large differences of population in the middle ranges.

We find a similar situation among the county boroughs. Birmingham has a population of well over a million, Liverpool nearly three-quarters of a million, while Canterbury has slightly over thirty thousand, Dudley below sixty-five thousand, Gloucester seventy thousand. The non-county boroughs range from towns like Swindon, Cambridge and Poole, all approaching the hundred thousand mark, or Rhondda which has just exceeded it, to tiny places with less than two thousand souls like Bishops Castle in Shropshire, Eye in Suffolk or Appleby in Westmorland. The urban districts range from Basildon with a population of 103,000 to Saxmundham with only 1,500; from Thurrock with 117,150 to Lynton with 1,680. Similar anomalies occur among the rural districts, which include in their ranks Chesterfield with a population of 104,130 at one end of the scale and Easington with 1,460 at the other.

There are similar disparities of territorial size. There are very large administrative counties like Devon (1,649,401 acres) and quite small ones such as the Holland Division of Lincolnshire (267,847 acres). Among the non-county boroughs we find Keighley with 23,640 acres and Woodstock with only 157 acres. Much the same applies to the urban and rural districts.

TABLE III: AREAS OF COUNCILS IN ACRES

Territorial Size	Number and Type of Local Authorities
Below 1,000 acres	11 Non-county borough councils 40 Urban district councils
1,000–1,999 acres	43 Non-county borough councils 87 Urban district councils
2,000–2,999 acres	1 County borough council 43 Non-county borough councils 80 Urban district councils 2 Rural district councils
3,000–4,999 acres	11 County borough councils 73 Non-county borough councils 143 Urban district councils 2 Rural district councils

Territorial Size	Number and Type of Local Authorities
5,000–9,999 acres	41 County borough councils 83 Non-county borough councils 128 Urban district councils 5 Rural district councils
10,000–14,999 acres	13 County borough councils 10 Non-county borough councils 23 Urban district councils 5 Rural district councils
15,000–19,999 acres	7 County borough councils 5 Non-county borough councils 21 Urban district councils 9 Rural district councils
20,000–29,999 acres	6 County borough councils 5 Non-county borough councils 4 Urban district councils 38 Rural district councils
30,000 plus acres	3 County borough councils 2 Urban district councils 405 Rural district councils

(Excluding County Councils and the GLC Area.) (Source: *Municipal Year Book*, 1965.)

We would not expect to find even approximate uniformity of size among the local authorities in each category, but such vast inequalities as these show that the municipal structure is utterly irrational. There must be a maximum and a minimum size of local authority for the effective and efficient performance of any specified group of functions; and whatever these may be, many existing authorities surely do not fall within them.

In short, a large proportion of local councils are not able to perform with tolerable efficiency and economy the functions they may reasonably be expected to discharge. Thus a county council should have not less than half-a-million population if it is to provide services at a satisfactory standard; but forty counties are below this figure and only eighteen are above it. For a county district the figure of 60,000 has been repeatedly laid down as the minimum population for giving a district council the right to have functions delegated to it by the county council covering a wide range of services, such as education, health, welfare and planning control.[1] Yet in 1964 only thirty-two districts, or one in twenty-six, reached this level.[2]

Turning to county boroughs, the statutory figure which is 'presumed' to be sufficient 'to support the discharge of the functions of a county borough council' is 100,000.[3] This figure is of doubtful validity. It merely crystallizes the outcome of the lengthy negotiations carried out between local authority associations over several years, and which involved a great deal of horse trading among vested interests. I am inclined to believe that a minimum figure of 200,000 is more realistic today than 100,000; and even this should not apply to the conurbations, in which much larger towns should be most-purpose rather than all-purpose authorities. The new London Boroughs have an average population of 250,000 and only four of them are below 200,000. The Home Office favour a population of not less than 200,000 mainly in order to be able to attract and retain staff of high quality;[4] and for police purposes the population should not be less than 250,000.[5]

The most important phenomenon of our time which has affected local government is that modern methods of transport have greatly increased the area of daily movement and enable large numbers of people to work in one area and live in another. The great cities draw their workpeople of all classes from housing estates, dormitory towns, and suburban, rural or semi-rural areas outside their boundaries. These people have to be provided with many services by the city in which they work, but most of them pay rates only to the council of the area in which they live.

The extension of the county borough form of government as it now exists is impracticable because if it were carried to its logical conclusion the counties would be left in a position of extreme weakness. Yet we need larger areas and authorities

[1] *Ante*, pp. 35–37.
[2] See *Municipal Year Book*, 1965, pp. 965, 1090, 1420.
[3] Local Government Act, 1958, Section 34.
[4] Report of the Royal Commission on Local Government in Greater London. Cmnd. 1164/1960, para 624.
[5] Final Report of the Royal Commission on the Police. Cmnd. 1728/1962, para 280.

for certain major services such as town and country planning, sewage disposal, technical education, traffic control, highways, housing, ambulances, fire brigades, police forces, etc.[1] and also smaller ones for purely local services. We need to combine urban, semi-urban and rural areas for some purposes. These aims can only be attained through a two-tier system.

The entire structure of local government needs to be re-modelled on new and bolder lines. Many or most of the county boroughs should be put back into the counties for a few major functions; and many of the counties should be drastically enlarged. It is useless to try to struggle on with the present pattern with only a little tinkering and patching here and there. As I shall show later on, however, this is what we are attempting to do—with the notable exception of Greater London, where a fundamental reform has been carried out.

[1] The Royal Commission on the Police reported in 1963 that the retention of forces numbering less than 350 in strength can be justified only by special circumstances. Moreover, they said that the optimum size of a force is much greater than this, and indicated a figure of 500 or more. As the police force appropriate to a population of 100,000 is about 200 on present standards, the minimum size laid down by the royal commission could and should lead to the amalgamation of a large number of county and county borough forces. Final Report Cmnd. 1728/1962, paras 279/280.

The Conservative Government accepted the principles recommended by the Royal Commission, and the Police Act, 1964, facilitates the creation of larger forces. Several amalgamations are now taking place.

XII

THE ATTITUDE OF LOCAL AUTHORITIES TO MUNICIPAL REFORM 1942–3

On the wider question of municipal reform, local authorities are also partly to blame for the present position. They have taken far too narrow a view of the situation and been far too occupied with the sectional interests of particular classes of local authority. The larger threat to local government as a whole has been almost overlooked.

During 1942 and 1943 each of the associations issued a report dealing with the problems of areas and organization.[1] There was general agreement among them that the existing organization of local government had a few defects and that the war-time system of Regional Commissioners must be abolished. Beyond this there was little or no agreement. The associations put forward widely differing proposals as to the kind of structure which is desirable, the proper distribution of powers and functions among authorities, the methods of creating urban and rural areas, the provision to be made for large-scale planning and administration, the number of tiers of authorities, the relations between the tiers and the optimum sizes of authorities.

To examine in detail the various proposals put forward by the associations in 1942–43 would at this stage serve no useful purpose. I shall therefore not attempt to do so here. The

[1] Final Report of the Executive Committee of the County Councils Association; Report of the Special Committee of the Association of Municipal Corporations adopted in July 1942; Report of the Urban District Councils Association on the Re-organization of Local Government, dated July 17, 1942; memorandum of the Executive Committee of the Rural District Councils Association, May 1942. Mention must also be made of the Interim Report of the NALGO Reconstruction Committee on the reform of Local Government Structure and the Report of the Labour Party on the Future of Local Government, though these two documents fall into a different category.

essential facts which emerged from these reports was that the associations spoke with discordant voices; that each class of local authority was playing for its own hand and that there was no effort to get together in order to formulate proposals which would benefit local government as a whole. Each association of local authorities identified its sectional interests with the welfare of the nation.

The NALGO Report, containing the views of an independent committee of the Association, also favoured the idea of setting up all-purpose authorities throughout the country, but advocated in addition the creation of provincial councils to exercise planning and co-ordinating functions for the services requiring large-scale treatment. These provincial councils would not possess executive powers; and the committee expressly declared that it did not envisage any organ of local government at the regional level, since this would be entirely unsuited to local government. Nevertheless, the acceptance of provincial councils for planning and co-ordination was an advance on the purely negative attitude of the associations of local authorities.

XIII

THE LABOUR PARTY'S REPORT 1943

The Labour Party boldly embraced the principle of regionalism. Their Report proposed the creation of a series of regional or major authorities whose areas would be sufficiently large to have adequate resources and to provide large-scale services but not so large as to lose any sense of common interest among the inhabitants of the region. These regional authorities would have extensive planning and administrative powers. Below the region would probably be 'an adaptation of the existing county areas, with amalgamations and absorptions of existing authorities, where necessary, to achieve a satisfactory unit'. Each region would thus contain a number of area authorities to administer purely local services and others delegated to them by the major authority.

It is worth noticing, in the light of subsequent events, the special emphasis laid by the Labour Party Report on the value of local government as 'an essential part of the framework of our democracy'. The Committee declared that 'the democratic tradition in local government is very powerful and nowhere more so than in the ranks of the Labour Movement. It is', they continued, 'not enough merely to affirm this principle.' Efforts must be made to translate Labour's ideas and ideals into 'a constructive system of government that will conform to the necessities of historical development'.[1] Suitable machinery should be set up by the central government to survey the country as a whole in order to determine the areas suitable for a regional or major authority, adequate for the efficient performance of large-scale services.

[1] *The Future of Local Government*, published by the Labour Party. (1943), pp. 7–8.

XIV

THE COALITION WHITE PAPER
ON LOCAL GOVERNMENT 1945

The Coalition Government, influenced by the lack of agreement among the associations, ran away from the whole problem. The White Paper on 'Local Government in England and Wales during the Period of Reconstruction', issued at the beginning of 1945, is mainly an escapist document.[1]

It opens with a statement made by the then Minister of Health in reply to a question in the House of Commons on August 3, 1944, in which he said that the reports from the associations had shown there to be 'no general desire to disrupt the existing structure of local government or to abandon in favour of some form of regional government the main features of the county and county borough system; and the Government do not consider that any case has been made out for so drastic a change'. On the other hand the Government were satisfied that there was need and scope for improvements within the general framework of the county and county borough system.[2]

The reasons which had led the Coalition Government to the view that the time is not opportune for a general recasting of the local government structure were twofold. First, the lack of any 'general desire in local government circles for a disruption of the present system, or any consensus of opinion as to what should replace it; and secondly, that the making of a change of this magnitude, which would by common consent have to be preceded by a full-dress inquiry, would be a process occupying some years and would seriously delay the establishment of the new or extended housing, educational, health and other services which form part of the Government's programme'.[3]

The White Paper acknowledged the contention that certain services need to be planned or administered over wider areas;

---

[1] Cmd. 6579/1945. H.M.S.O.   [2] *Ibid.*, p. 2.   [3] *Ibid.*, p. 4.

and that the reconstruction programme would place an impossible burden on local government finance. But it did not regard either of these arguments as sufficient reason for introducing fundamental reforms. As regards the former, it examined in turn various alternative ways in which wider areas could be obtained for certain services. These include nationalization, regionalization and the creation of joint authorities.[1]

So far as nationalization was concerned, the Government declared themselves to be opposed to 'any general policy of centralizing services hitherto regarded as essentially local'. They were, however, not prepared to rule out altogether the possibility of transferring certain functions if on the merits of the case this course should be shown to be desirable.[2] Regionalism in the form of directly elected councils to administer certain services was dismissed in eight lines for no apparent reason other than the opposition of the associations. The third alternative of joint boards or committees formed of local authorities co-operating for particular purposes was therefore regarded as offering the best remedy in present circumstances. Hence, the White Paper declared the Government's intention of relying on the existing structure based on the county and county borough, with appropriate machinery, where necessary, for combined action.[3]

The White Paper was in many ways a highly misleading document. In the first place, it presented the case for reform as though it were a proposal to 'disrupt' an inherently stable and sound structure. In point of fact this was directly contrary to the truth. The present system is rapidly disintegrating through the loss of functions and through being by-passed in regard to new activities. This process is occurring because the structure is ramshackle and obsolete. The only chance of preserving and strengthening local government is by means of a fundamental improvement in the structure. It is in this light that proposals for reform should be regarded.

In the second place, the disavowal of any 'general policy' of centralizing local services evaded the issue. It does not matter in the least whether hospitals, public utilities, main roads and

---

[1] Cmd. 6579/1945. H.M.S.O., p. 4.   [2] *Ibid.*, p. 5.   [3] *Ibid.*, p. 6.

public assistance services are transferred to central departments or to public boards or corporations as a matter of 'general policy' or merely as a piece-meal expedient adopted in each case. The result is exactly the same. What matters is the loss of power, interest and responsibility, and the decline of democratic local government, which these transfers must cause.

Thirdly, the excessive deference shown to the associations of local authorities and their implied identification with the public interest resulted in the whole picture being out of perspective. The White Paper referred to the opposition to change of 'local government circles' without either describing their nature or analysing the validity of their objections. It simply accepted the opposition of these unnamed 'circles' as a conclusive argument in favour of a policy of inaction.

The expression 'local government circles' is, presumably, only another name for the associations of local authorities. Even a cursory glance at these bodies shows that they represent particular categories of local authorities and are therefore unlikely or unable to take a comprehensive and disinterested view of the position. They have invariably played the part of defence organs for the sectional interests of their members.

It was utterly wrong for the White Paper and for the Government—both then and subsequently—to identify the national interest in a vigorous and healthy local government system with the partial views of such bodies. Local government exists for the benefit of the nation as a whole, and of the local communities into which it is divided. The task of the central government and of Parliament should be to determine the general framework within which local authorities can administer services in an effective and democratic manner. To consider the councillors, the councils and their associations instead of the citizens and their communities is a fundamental mistake. Moreover, the central government must lead in this matter, not merely follow and obey the views of local authorities. That was the attitude which produced the Municipal Corporations Act, 1835, the Local Government Acts of 1888 and 1894, and all the other great improvements of the past century as well as the recent reforms in Greater London. There would have been no major reforms in the nineteenth century if the government of the day had taken the wishes of 'local government circles' as their guide. It is odd that while the central government has not hesitated to curtail unduly the freedom and independence of local authorities in their day to day administration, in this matter of organization and structure, which is essentially a question of national policy, the central government is subservient and reluctant to interfere.

XV

THE LOCAL GOVERNMENT
BOUNDARY COMMISSION 1945–49

The one constructive proposal contained in the White Paper was the creation of a Local Government Boundary Commission. The suggestion originated in the reports of the National Association of Local Government Officers and of the Labour Party. Both these bodies envisaged a Commission with very wide powers to review existing local government areas and authorities. The White Paper took a narrower view of the functions proper to such a body. Its powers were to comprise those hitherto exercised by county councils and the Minister of Health in regard to the review of county districts prescribed by the Local Government Act, 1933; the creation and extensions of county boroughs; the demotion of small county boroughs to non-county borough status; and the union of contiguous county boroughs and some of the smaller administrative counties.[1]

This narrower conception was embodied in the Local Government (Boundary Commission) Act, 1945. The statute provided for the establishment of a Boundary Commission charged with the duty of reviewing the circumstances of the areas into which England and Wales (exclusive of the administrative County of London) were divided for the purposes of local government, and exercising, where it appeared to the Commission expedient so to do, the powers of altering these areas conferred by the Act.[2] The Commission consisted of a chairman, deputy chairman, and three other members, who were paid salaries and allowances determined by the Treasury. The Commission appointed its own staff subject to Treasury approval and consultation with the Minister of Health.

The Commission was given statutory power to alter or define

---

[1] Cmd. 6579/1945. H.M.S.O., p. 12.   [2] Section I (1).

the boundaries of a county, county borough or county district. It could unite a county with another county, or combine one county borough with another county borough. It could amalgamate non-county boroughs. It could marry county districts of any kind or include them in a county borough. It could promote a borough (enlarged, if necessary, by the accession of adjoining territory) to county borough status. It could demote a county borough to non-county borough rank. It could carve up a county into two or more counties, or eliminate it by dividing its territory between or among two or more other counties. It could dispose of urban or rural districts in a similar fashion.[1]

Neither Parliament nor the Minister attempted to lay down any general policy for the Commission or to indicate the broad outlines of the structure which it was to promote. There were, however, four negative injunctions: (1) The exclusion of the Administrative County of London from the purview of the Commission. (2) A prohibition on the creation of county boroughs in Middlesex. (3) The fixing of a population level of 60,000 as a maximum limit for the reduction in rank of county boroughs to non-county borough status. (4) The fixing of a population level of 100,000 as a maximum for the elimination of county councils.

The idea of creating a Commission to deal with questions of local government areas and authorities was an excellent one. The method was, indeed, preferable to any which had hitherto been used for this task. It was less susceptible to political influences and far more expert than the Parliamentary Private Bill procedure, which had been necessary since 1926 for opposed applications for the extension or creation of county boroughs. It could bring to the settlement of county district problems a wider view than any county council is likely to possess. The ultimate control by Parliament was assured by requiring that orders made by the Commission relating to a county or a county borough were provisional only and had no effect until confirmed by Parliament.[2] The Minister of Health's responsibility for local government was preserved by empowering him, after consulting the associations of local authorities concerned, to make regulations prescribing general principles

[1] Section 2.   [2] Section 3 (9).

by which the Commission were to be guided in the exercise of their functions. These regulations had to be affirmed by positive resolution of each House of Parliament.[1]

For the first time this century a compact body of able, experienced, disinterested, and independent commissioners was charged with the duty of reviewing the circumstances of the areas into which the country is divided for the purpose of local government and given extensive powers of improving those areas. They could take the initiative instead of merely arbitrating on claims put forward by one authority and opposed by another. They could undertake first-hand investigation in the field, instead of having to be content with highly-coloured evidence presented at a public enquiry by counsel for the contending parties.

Despite these advantages as an instrument of reform, the Commission was severely handicapped by the lack of two essential powers. One was that it had no jurisdiction over functions. The other was that it was unable to create new types of authorities exercising powers over regional areas. It could not, for example, combine one or more county boroughs with neighbouring county councils, or establish a regional authority over them for specified purposes. Nor could it create a Greater Manchester County Council with a two-tier system of authorities similar to that obtaining in London. Another important limit to the scope of the Commission was the exclusion of Scotland from its jurisdiction.

[1] Section 1 (3).

XVI

THE BOUNDARY COMMISSION'S
PROPOSALS 1947

The main contribution of the Local Government Boundary Commission is contained in its report for the year 1947. This report was the first sign from any official body which indicated either the parlous state into which local government has fallen or the kind of changes which are necessary to effect even a partial recovery. The Report was a brief and business-like document. It made no attempt to trace the historical development of the present condition, nor did it attribute blame or criticism for what had occurred. It wasted no words on eloquence. Its essential purpose was to describe shortly the causes of weakness in local government and to prescribe remedies.

The weaknesses, the Commissioners pointed out, are due to the disparity in size and resources of individual counties, county boroughs, and county districts; the failure of the local government system to adapt itself to the changing pattern of modern industrial England, particularly in the case of the great conurbations in the Black Country, Manchester, Merseyside, Tyneside, the West Riding, Tees-side, and elsewhere; the increased central control which has deprived local authorities of a large measure of their independence; the haphazard allocation of functions among local authorities on a piecemeal basis; and, above all, the conflict between county councils and county borough councils which has arisen from the constant pressure on the part of the big towns to extend their boundaries and the desire of non-county boroughs to acquire county borough status. This conflict between town and county has been gnawing at the vitals of local government with increasing intensity for half a century.

The Commission recognised that in towns of certain types and sizes, one-tier government is preferable and that elsewhere the two-tier system should prevail. It was in their application of this principle that the Commission departed largely from the existing arrangements.

They recommended that henceforth the whole of England and Wales should be divided into counties, each with its own county council. Most of the present counties would continue unchanged as major authorities, though some of the smallest counties would be merged with others and the largest ones divided. There would, in addition, be a number of new counties consisting of large cities and towns, sometimes associated with the surrounding urban, rural or semi-rural environs. These new counties would in some instances have one-tier administration (and would therefore resemble the present county boroughs), while in others there would be a two-tier form of local government. The general aim would be to provide a population of between 200,000 and 1,000,000 for each new two-tier county, and a population of 200,000 to 500,000 for every new single-tier county.

County boroughs would not disappear, but they would no longer be entirely separate from the administrative county for all local government purposes. What the Commission called 'new county boroughs' would form a new category of lower-tier authorities which would have a superior position to county district councils, but would form part of the county for certain purposes. They would (unlike county districts) be autonomous local authorities for education, health and medical services, the care of the aged and disabled, and perhaps the care of children deprived of a normal home life. They would be authorised to claim responsibility for executing the repair, maintenance and construction of classified highways though the finance of these highways would be a county council function. They would have a separate commission of the peace, a coroner and a sheriff, and discharge the duties relating to the adminis-tration of justice. They would prepare the detailed plans for their own areas within the framework of the town and country plan prepared by the county council. They would be given all the functions at present performed by the largest non-county boroughs in regard to housing, reconstruction areas, slum clearance, town improvements, sewerage and sewage disposal, allotments, libraries, museums and art galleries, civic restaurants, food and drugs, cemeteries and crematoria, mortuaries, parks, open spaces and playing fields, baths and wash-houses and many other matters.

The principal differences which would exist between a new county borough and the present ones is that the county council and not the county borough council would be responsible for the main town and country plan, for the police force, the fire service, land drainage, small holdings, remand homes, approved schools, road fund and local taxation licences, the diseases of animals and the finance of highways. Thus the largest and wealthiest towns would be brought into the county system for a few purposes. They would continue to exercise autonomous powers over a wide range of local government functions. They were described in the Report as 'most-purpose' authorities, to distinguish them from the county district councils, which do not have so large a degree of responsibility, and the all-purpose county boroughs of today.

All the major organs of local government would have been called counties; but in addition there would be county boroughs, which would form part of the county for certain purposes. When the Commission reported there were forty-nine county councils and eighty county borough councils in England. Under their scheme there would have been sixty-seven counties, of which forty-seven would be two-tier and twenty one-tier together with sixty-three county boroughs.

The Local Government Boundary Commission's proposals had considerable merits and some serious defects. They would have greatly diminished the ceaseless conflict between the existing county and county borough councils, although much hostility would have remained. They would have secured the abolition of the obviously unfit units of local government. On the other hand, they made no attempt whatever to make provision for large-scale planning and administration.

The Commissioners never for a moment turned their eyes towards the regional movement which has wrought havoc with local government. They did not ask why responsibility for electricity and gas supply, hospitals, trunk roads, passenger road services, and other services has been taken away from local authorities and given to regional or central bodies; or under what conditions it might be practicable for these functions to be restored to the realm of local self-government. The Commissioners apparently accepted as a *fait accompli* the deplorable state of diminished power, interest and responsibility in which local government finds itself at present, without diagnosing the underlying causes or seeking a fundamental remedy.

Yet surely there are some extremely important lessons to be learnt from recent events. It is not an accident that the public utility, road transport and hospital services require regional administration and planning. Nor is it far-fetched to assume that if local government could be projected on to a regional scale, and elected councils set up covering the regional areas which technical reasons render necessary for public utility services, town and country planning, hospital administration and other services, it would be practicable to demand a reversal of current centralizing trends. If there were an available alternative to centralization, and the creation of appointed *ad hoc* bodies, the outlook would be entirely changed.

Thus, while the report marked a great advance on any previous official document on the subject, it did not go far enough. Its policy of restoring the county borough to the county was sound in principle but its proposals were half-hearted. Its fear of being accused of recommending regionalism led it to ignore the whole regional problem. The areas of circulation for economic and social purposes have expanded owing to further development in transport and communications, and the 'areas of consciousness' have become more regional in character. The progress of thought in the physical planning movement has moved towards the closer integration of town and country life. In consequence, the administrative dichotomy embodied in the Local Government Act, 1888, which introduced the distinction between county council and county borough, is an outworn conception. Proper areas cannot be obtained by any simple combination of county boroughs and county councils. Finally, full-length studies of the metropolitan region[1] show that it is hopeless to expect a high degree of co-operation between county borough and county councils.

[1] W. A. Robson: *The Government and Misgovernment of London* (2nd ed.) 1948. See also *Great Cities of the World: Their Government, Politics and Planning.* Ed. by W. A. Robson (2nd ed.) 1957.

XVII

Mr ANEURIN BEVAN AND LOCAL GOVERNMENT REFORM

The late Mr Aneurin Bevan was Minister of Health in the Labour Government from 1945 to 1950, and during that period his department was responsible for the general well-being of local government. In the Local Government Boundary Commission, Mr Bevan had at hand a new and promising instrument for effective reform. He was, moreover, in a position to foster, guide or hinder reform in a quite decisive way, for the Minister of Health was empowered to make regulations prescribing the general principles by which the Commission were to be guided. Unfortunately, Mr Bevan neither grasped the opportunities open to him nor was willing to devote time and energy to the matter. His address to the conference of the Association of Municipal Associations in 1946 set the keynote for all his subsequent actions. His speech on that occasion was a model of evasion. After explaining that some functions have transcended the old organs of local government and that the local government instrument has therefore become inadequate, Mr Bevan disclaimed any responsibility for the situation thus revealed. 'It is not a matter for me,' he said, 'I throw the charge back.' In short, the Government had to assume the obsolete character of local government areas and authorities as something permanent and irremediable, and on that basis merely decide whether or not particular services should be entrusted to them or diverted elsewhere. In adopting this attitude, Mr Bevan virtually relinquished his constitutional responsibility for the general well-being of local goverment.

The extreme lethargy and indifference with which he viewed the problem was revealed by his attitude towards a resolution before the Conference asking for an investigation into the structure of local government. He simply dismissed this with the statement that it would have to be preceded by an investigation into the kind of society in which local government must find its place. As the functions were undergoing considerable change and 'we do not know what context local government is going to live in, it does not seem to me to be an appropriate time for an enquiry of that sort'. Considering that the Labour Government was in process of carrying out a vast programme of economic and social reconstruction, one would have thought the then Minister of Health would have known better than most people the emerging shape of the welfare state. One would also have thought the moment singularly propitious for an enquiry into the role of local government in that state, rather than to wait until local authorities have been deprived of their powers, shorn of their independence, undermined and by-passed in many different ways, before beginning an investigation which would largely be a post-mortem.

Mr Bevan had begun his speech by assuring his audience that they need have 'no misgivings about the general attitude of the Government towards local government'. Later in his address Mr Bevan observed that local authorities were naturally jealous and apprehensive at losing functions, and he assured them that additional functions would be given to them in order to maintain the vitality and importance of local government. He ended by declaring his belief that local government has an even more glorious future than its past and expressed his conviction that 'we are going to broaden its functions and enrich its administration and add to its significance in the social life of our people'. In the meantime, the Boundary Commission would make such adaptations as are necessary in the transition period.

The following year the Local Government Boundary Commission made their principal report described above.[1] The Commission pointed out that they had reached the conclusion that in many areas their powers and instructions did not permit the formation of local government units as effective and convenient as they should be. Faced with a choice between making second-best modifications in the existing system within the limits of their powers or of explaining their proposals for more

[1] Report of the Local Government Boundary Commission for 1947. H.M.S.O.

far-reaching reconstruction, they decided to choose the latter alternative. 'If our recommendations commend themselves, some legislative action and some amendment of the general principles (laid down by the Minister in his regulations) will be necessary. If they do not, it will be our duty to proceed to carry out our task on the basis of the present instructions, but in that case we should necessarily reconsider many of the regroupings of units recommended in this Report.'

The Commissioners had devoted much of their report to the functions of local authorities, although they had no jurisdiction to consider powers. In this they shared the view which Mr Bevan had expressed in Parliament that it is nonsensical to attempt to discuss local authority boundaries without also talking about functions and *vice versa*.

The 1947 Report of the Local Government Boundary Commission was virtually their swan song. Shortly afterwards Mr Bevan announced in Parliament that he intended to abolish the Commission and this was carried out in 1949. In the debate on the Local Government Boundary Commission (Dissolution) Bill, Mr Bevan explained that he had been driven to take this step by the lack of support among local authorities for the Commission's proposals, and by the inadequacy of their powers. Thus ended a promising experiment which might have produced good results if the Minister had supported the Commission and asked Parliament to enlarge their powers so that they could reform local government more comprehensively. Instead he took the reactionary step of restoring the sterile and obstructive Private Bill procedure for effecting alterations of areas. This deplorable step was accompanied by the usual expression of faith in the virtues of local government which has become common form with Ministers who intend to do nothing to help it overcome the deep-seated malaise from which it is suffering.

These ineluctable facts are set out in order to show that Mr Bevan, who was widely regarded as a Labour leader of radical left-wing views, revealed no traces of any zeal for radical reform of local government nor any strong belief in its virtues. His attitude of neglect and indifference towards local government was characteristic of the outlook of the Labour Party as a whole during the period after 1945 when serious amputations have taken place in the functions of local authorities. A symptom of this is that the Labour Party's Election Manifesto for the 1964 Election contained no mention of local government as a subject in its own right. It was mentioned only in connection with regional planning boards which would 'work closely with representatives of the local authorities, both sides of industry and other interests in the region'.

XVIII

THE PROPOSALS OF FOUR ASSOCIATIONS OF LOCAL AUTHORITIES 1953

After the dissolution of the Local Government Boundary Commission the Association of Municipal Corporations, the County Councils Association, and the associations representing urban districts and rural districts decided to confer together to see if they could agree upon a scheme of local government reform for submission to the Government. In May 1952 the Association of Municipal Corporations withdrew from these discussions and the National Association of Parish Councils was invited to participate in them. In March 1953 a report was issued containing the proposals and recommendations agreed by the representatives of the County Councils Association, the Urban District Councils Association, the Rural District Councils Association, and the National Association of Parish Councils.

The joint report of the four associations consisted of a short introductory statement followed by an appendix containing the recommendations. We were surprised to learn from the former that members of both Houses of Parliament are 'intensely interested in the reorganization of local government'. This good news had indeed been kept secret for an unduly long time. An even more astonishing remark was that 'the existing framework of local government has proved to be not only satisfactory but also so flexible as to be capable of modification and evolution without the necessity of any alteration of structure. The proposals are therefore based upon the existing types of local authorities.' Would that these observations were true! For in that event local government would not be in the parlous state in which it now finds itself.

The report assumed the continuance of a system of two-tier

government within conurbations and administrative counties (with parish councils forming a third tier in rural districts); and one-tier government elsewhere. But the existing administrative counties were not to be regarded as sacrosanct, and the Ministry of Housing and Local Government would be asked to conduct a general review of county boundaries, for the first time since they were established in 1888. The Minister would be authorized to divide, amalgamate, alter and extend administrative counties in order to ensure that they are made, individually and collectively, effective and convenient units of local government.

County boroughs with a population of less than 75,000 would revert to non-county borough status. This would affect nineteen county boroughs, including Chester, Canterbury, Barrow-in-Furness, Lincoln, Eastbourne, Hastings, Worcester, Bury and Burton-on-Trent.

Non-county boroughs and urban districts would not be entitled to apply for county borough status unless they have a population of 100,000 or more. Even then they must not lie within a conurbation. Of the thirteen non-county boroughs and three urban districts which satisfied the population condition only two—the Borough of Luton and the Urban District of Rhondda—would be eligible for county borough status, since all the others were situated in the Greater London area.

The proposals affecting conurbations were extremely vague. Parliament would be asked to define by statute the boundaries of the great conurbations. These conurbations would then be reviewed by the Minister of Housing and Local Government, who would draw up and submit to Parliament for approval schemes defining the authorities to be established in each conurbation and the distribution of functions between them. No hint was given as to the number, size, or character of the conurbations, nor was there any indication of the form of government which was contemplated for them except that it would be a two-tier system.

Without knowing what was intended it is impossible to express any opinion on the merits of this crucial feature of the report. For in effect all that it said was: Let there be conurbations. Let Parliament define them. And let the Minister create a two-tier system of local government for them. It is possible that the associations considered this problem to be too difficult and contentious for them to solve; and that in consequence they thought it best to leave it to the Minister and Parliament.

After the administrative counties had been reviewed by the Minister, the county councils would undertake a review of county districts on the lines authorized by the Local Government Acts of 1929 and 1933, except that boroughs and districts would be treated alike for this purpose.

XIX

THE ATTITUDE OF THE ASSOCIATION OF MUNICIPAL CORPORATIONS

The reaction of the Association of Municipal Corporations was prompt, forcible and wholly unfavourable. The Association would have nothing whatever to do with the report.[1] They declined to pay even a conventional tribute to two-tier local government, which they regard as a second-best form even in those areas where it may be necessary. They refused to accept the proposal that any existing county boroughs should lose status or functions; and they not only opposed the 75,000 population minimum but contended that it should be lowered to 50,000. Even in the conurbations the Association of Municipal Corporations were quite unable to see why areas should be denied the advantages of all-purpose authorities. If in any conurbation it should be found necessary to transcend the county borough council which is part of the Providential Plan for the blessing of mankind, any arrangements made to facilitate planning or administration in larger areas should be regarded as exceptions to the general principle that county borough government is the best form and should prevail wherever possible.

The observations of the Association on the Report drawn up by the four other associations made no attempt to conceal the blatant fact that the Association of Municipal Corporations is primarily and, so far as one can see, exclusively concerned to promote the special interests of municipal corporations. Again and again they considered proposals in the report purely from the point of view of their effect on boroughs.

Having recorded their complete opposition to the report of

---

[1] See the Observations on the Report of the Reorganization of Local Government Sub-Committee of the General Purposes Committee, Association of Municipal Corporations, published on June 16, 1953.

the four associations, the Association's only positive gesture was to bring out of cold storage their own reorganization scheme, adopted on July 23, 1942. This scheme, by that time eleven years old, was based on the erroneous belief that after the war the scope of local government services would be extended. It proceeded on the assumption that the county borough type of organ should be established wherever possible. 'The most satisfactory form of local government', they said, 'is for most areas a single authority invested with complete powers of local government within its area.' The differentiation between local government in urban and in rural areas which has hitherto prevailed has been carried too far, and the Association of Municipal Corporations sees no reason why the county borough should not comprise both rural and urban areas under the jurisdiction of a single council. This would involve extending county borough boundaries to include very large areas of rural or semi-rural, or mixed urban and rural, territory in the environment of the larger towns. The desirability of this course was argued on the ground that rural areas are not financially able to provide all the local government services they need without the help of urban areas. Nothing was said of the disadvantage of governing remote villages and rural communities, not to mention isolated urban districts, with a genuine life of their own, from the town hall of a big city many miles away; or the destruction of community values which this would involve.

The inclusion within its membership of both county borough councils and non-county borough councils has induced the Association of Municipal Corporations to advocate single-tier local government as the only policy likely to appeal to both classes of members—on the assumption that the larger non-county boroughs would all like to attain county borough status.

The reasons put forward in favour of a one-tier system by the AMC are: (1) the simpler the structure, the more likely it is to be understood and to work well. (2) Powers should be conferred directly on the authority which administers a service and should be exercised as of right and not by way of delegation. (3) One body of elected councillors should be answerable to the electorate so that responsibility is one and undivided. (4) The authority that raises revenue should be entrusted with its expenditure.[1]

Each of these 'maxims' of good local government not only extols the virtues of county boroughs but gives a side kick at the alleged defects of the county system.

The Association of Municipal Corporations is not prepared to concede the need for any other form of structure even in the conurbations, which are 'in danger of receiving undue prominence in discussions on the reorganization of local government'.[2] The newspapers are accused of concentrating on the conurbations and calling for changes in the manner of providing services therein without considering the fact that they are run very well at present in those areas.[3]

In any event the AMC would not allow its political position to be undermined by an excessive regard for administrative efficiency and convenience. A close relationship between the electorate and their representatives is essential to democratic government and this can be best assured by the one-tier system. No other consideration must be allowed to overshadow this supreme virtue.[4]

The AMC has been nonetheless ready to urge the creation of larger areas of local government—so long as they are administered by municipal corporations. Thus, its reply to the report of the four other associations included a proposal for the merger of urban and rural areas to produce county districts of at least 50,000 population.[5] Amalgamation is necessary to enable district councils to retain their remaining powers; and wherever possible urban-rural unification should take the form of a county borough. If this were not possible, the county council should control only planning and co-ordination.[6]

A long-standing grievance of the Association is that the financial difficulties of the counties have been used 'to prevent the proper government of the expanded areas of county

---

[1] Reorganization of Local Government. A.M.C. Report (April 1954), para 51. See *Municipal Review*, July 1954, Supplement, pp. 153–54.

[2] *Ibid.*, September 1954, Supplement, pp. 143–44.

[3] *Municipal Review*, October 1956, pp. 185–86.   [4] *Ibid.*, March 1961, p. 141.

[5] Reorganization of Local Government. A.M.C. Report (April 1954), para 51. See *Municipal Review*, July 1954, Supplement, pp. 153–54.

[6] *Ibid.*, October 1954, p. 163.

boroughs'.[1] This was a reference to boundary extensions desired by county boroughs.

Despite its policy of enlarging county districts the Association has also been under pressure from some of its members to protect the many very small boroughs whose life might be threatened if reform were undertaken on a serious scale. For example, a resolution was passed at the Annual Conference in 1960 urging the AMC to take all possible steps to ensure the continuance in being of the small country town boroughs. The Association was asked to press the Government to reconsider their apparent policy of judging local government matters in counties by the test of what is best for the county council.[2]

The AMC has never shown the slightest concern for the well-being of county government. Indeed, the Association has on occasion said it would like to see it disappear even in purely rural areas not containing any important town.[3]

This extreme preoccupation with the narrow interests of their members has led the Association to adopt a position which was hopelessly unrealistic. In all the protracted discussions, public and private, official and unofficial, on local government reform during the past forty years, no one outside the AMC has seriously supported the notion of having a single-tier system throughout the country.

One result of persistently advocating an unrealistic policy has been to reduce the influence of the Association when these questions are under discussion. Members of the Association in their more reflective moments are doubtless aware of this.

When the White Paper on *Areas and Status of Local Authorities* was issued in 1956 the AMC declared that its outstanding merit was the recognition 'that the boroughs must be

---

[1] See *Municipal Review*, October 1954.   [2] *Ibid.*, November 1960, p. 709.

[3] In a statement issued by the General Purposes Committee prior to a special general meeting of the AMC held on July 23, 1942, the Committee explained that although in some instances it might be unavoidably necessary for the county council to become the all-purpose authority in an agricultural area not containing any important town, the Committee 'have always contemplated that, in the majority of cases, the functions and areas of existing county councils would be severely reduced and possibily, in some instances, entirely abolished, and a unit of government other than the county council, would eventually become the all-purposes authority'. The Association has expressed similar views on several subsequent occasions.

allowed to expand'.[1] The subsequent White Paper on *Functions of County and District Councils* was a source of 'profound dissatisfaction' to the Association in that (1) it abandoned the idea of conferring powers directly on non-county boroughs and withdrew some powers which were already conferred; (2) it proposed to delegate more functions to district councils despite the well-known objections of non-county boroughs to delegation; (3) it adoped a uniform standard of 60,000 for automatic delegation irrespective of the nature and requirements of the services concerned.[2] Moreover, the White Paper elevated delegation 'from an unwelcome expedient to a desirable objective'.[3]

The 1958 Local Government Act registered a further reverse for the AMC. The proposed reorganization envisaged in the Bill, the *Municipal Review* admitted, 'is not the pattern which the Association advocated'. The one- and two-tier systems had been maintained virtually intact.[4]

[1] *Municipal Review*, October 1956, p. 186.
[2] *Ibid.*, August 1957, p. 327.   [3] *Ibid.*, July 1957, p. 283.
[4] *Ibid.*, January 1958, p. 9.

XX

THE ATTITUDE OF THE
COUNTY COUNCILS ASSOCIATION

The County Councils Association has shared the complacency of the Association of Municipal Corporations in regard to the conurbations. Thus, its evidence to the Royal Commission on Local Government in Greater London defended the county councils concerned by stating that 'the existing arrangements work reasonably well',[1]—which they certainly did not. When the Herbert report was published the County Councils Association criticized it on the ground that a Greater London Council was too large to be considered as local government at all.[2]

The attitude of the CCA throughout the post-war period has been on the whole sluggish and conservative. It has not been chasing shadows in the manner of the AMC—its members were mainly anxious to preserve the *status quo*—and at no stage has it advanced any idea which could be called radical. It has been content to let things jog along as they are unless a danger from without appeared to threaten county government, such as the Greater London reforms, the creation of the Regional Planning Boards and Councils, and more recently the prospect of numerous non-county boroughs attaining a population of 100,000. Any form of regionalism has always been anathema to the County Councils Association. The most they would concede has been the formation of joint authorities. The Association has not attacked the one-tier system in principle but accepts the notion that large and growing towns must be accorded county borough status after a certain point of development has been reached. One of the few occasions for opposing the single-tier system was when the Association criticized the idea of handing over Greater London to a group of county boroughs. But it

---

[1] *County Councils Association Gazette*, June 1959, Supplement, p. 131.
[2] *Ibid.*, March 1961, Supplement, p. 98.

also rejected the notion of a directly elected metropolitan authority for the whole metropolis.[1]

The cca gave qualified approval to the White Paper on *Areas and Status*.[2] It accepted in principle most of the provisions of the 1957 Local Government Bill, though seeking modification on particular points. It expressed satisfaction at the fact that the Bill did not contain provisions for the delegation or further delegation of any county services beyond those of education, health and welfare.[3] On the other hand, it viewed with regret the absence of a provision to abolish the divisional executives.[4]

The county councils have been and still are in a more favourable position than the county boroughs because the increase in population and rateable value of the large towns has occurred mainly outside the city limits. In consequence, whereas the amc has had to face the problem of maintaining the relative position of the county boroughs *vis-à-vis* the county councils, an end which could be achieved only by the extension of county borough boundaries or the creation of new county boroughs, the cca has merely had to resist changes in area or status in order to achieve relative growth.

Very recently, however, the cca has become aware of a serious potential danger to the stability of county government in the large increases of population which are now forecast for the remaining decades of the present century. The revised estimates of population growth vastly exceed those made in 1955, and the cca fears that a large number of non-county boroughs and urban districts will in consequence exceed the figure of 100,000 which is now laid down as the basic qualification for eligibility for county borough status. The cca contends not only that the 100,000 benchmark is now quite insufficient to enable small county boroughs to perform effectively such functions as planning, education, and the provision of a police force; but that to act on the statutory presumption

[1] *County Councils Association Gazette*, June 1959, Supplement, pp. 131–34.

[2] *Ibid.*, January 1957. Report of General Purposes Committee. Supplement, pp. 28–29, 32–38.

[3] C.C.A. Annual Report, 1957, in *C.C.A. Gazette* May 1958, p. 139.

[4] *C.C.A. Gazette*, December 1957, p. 241.

that county borough status shall be conferred on towns which attain that figure will disrupt county government to a disastrous extent. The Association therefore calls for a revision of the Local Government Act, 1958.

In a memorandum prepared for the Minister of Housing and Local Government the c c a proposed that the figure for full county borough status shall be raised to 175,000. Towns with populations between 100,000 and 175,000 should be eligible to become 'new county boroughs'. In that capacity they would have, in addition to all the functions possessed by county district councils, excepted district status in respect of education, and entire responsibility for the personal health, welfare and children's services; the local parts of town and country planning within the framework of the county plan, together with planning control; all roads within their areas except probably some specified major through-roads; and civil defence. The new county boroughs would form part of the counties in which they are situated for strategic planning, the police, fire and education services, ambulances, and major traffic regulation.[1]

This proposal will inevitably be strongly opposed by the A M C and the usual dogfight between the associations will ensue. But from an objective point of view the c c a is essentially right. Indeed, many disinterested students of local government are disposed to regard a population of 200,000 rather than 175,000 as the minimum qualification which should entitle a town to become an autonomous county borough for all purposes. But as I shall explain later, autonomous county boroughs are out of place in the conurbations and in the city regions.

The most adverse feature of British local government is not the dual system of one- and two-tier areas but the fact that the county councils and the borough councils were allowed to set up separate associations. These organizations have been solely concerned to defend the interests of their members without regard to the well-being of local government as a whole. 'They

[1] Memondandum on Local Government Reorganization in England, approved by the Executive Council of the C.C.A. on July 28, 1965 for submission to the Minister.

have a sorry record', Professor Keith-Lucas remarks, 'when it comes to shaping policy. In all the discussions before the Local Government Act of 1958 they devoted their principal efforts to attacking each other, like the Kilkenny cats. . . .'[1]

[1] 'The Too-narrow Powers of Council' in *Local Government Today and To-morrow* (Ed. Dudley Lofts), p. 32.

XXI

THE CONCORDAT 1956

With such a fundamental divergence of view expressed in these reports and attitudes there seemed to be little prospect of achieving a consensus among the associations. In November 1954 Mr Duncan Sandys, who had become Minister of Housing and Local Government the previous month, requested representatives of the five associations to meet him. He told them that the Government would not be prepared to undertake any substantial reform unless there was general agreement among the associations about the lines on which it should proceed. In his opinion the existing system had not broken down and he would not consider abolishing either the two-tier system in the counties or the single-tier system in the big towns. Having received this assurance that the Government did not intend doing anything drastic the representatives of the associations said that they did not want the question shelved for an indefinite period and they offered to try to reach agreement on the basis of the existing structure at a series of further meetings if the Minister would take the chair.

Thereafter the associations did agree upon a number of proposals which were published as an appendix to a White Paper entitled 'Area and Status of Local Authorities in England and Wales'. The matters which were admitted to require attention were: (1) the need to ensure that all local authorities are effective and convenient units of local government; (2) claims for boundary extensions by county boroughs; (3) claims by non-county boroughs and urban districts for county borough status; (4) the effects on counties of such claims for extensions and promotions; (5) the desire of county districts to exercise some of the functions being performed by county councils; (6) the improved organization of local government in the conurbations; and (7) the need to have a substantial standstill period after any necessary changes had been made.

On the question of the actual policies to be applied, the associations agreed that a county district with a population of 100,000 or more should be presumed to be able to discharge effectively and conveniently the functions of a county borough if it sought promotion to that status. On the other hand, a smaller authority should be required to show 'exceedingly good reason to justify promotion' both in terms of its own abilities and in regard to the effect which such promotion would have on the county as a whole. Where a county borough could be shown to be unable to discharge effectively and conveniently its functions owing to its small population, inadequate resources or for any other reason, its demotion to a lower status might be considered. Similarly, the division, amalgamation, alteration and extension of counties could where desirable be included in any reorganization. In the conurbations the aim should be to secure effective and convenient units of local government throughout each conurbation. The case for county borough creations and extensions should stand on the same footing as the need to ensure a proper organization of local government on a two-tier basis in those parts of the conurbation lying outside county boroughs. Subject to this, the minimum population for a county district seeking county borough status in a conurbation would be 125,000. Middlesex should be preserved as a two-tier county!

The concordat included a proposal for a statutory Local Government Commission to review counties, county boroughs and conurbations in England and a separate Commission for Wales. Their reports would be presented to the Minister and their recommendations embodied in Ministerial orders, with any amendments the Minister might choose to make, and be submitted by him to Parliament for approval or rejection. The agreement even included the precise procedure to be followed by the Commission, the Minister and Parliament.

Finally, the concordat dealt at length with the review of county districts by county councils. This could include the alteration of district boundaries and the making of recommendations to the Minister for dividing, extending, altering or amalgamating their areas, and for demoting non-county boroughs to urban districts. Functions were to be examined with a view to ensuring that they should be exercised 'at the lowest administrative level consistent with efficiency and economy'. The scope of delegated powers would be widened, and although nothing specific was promised, the general aim would be to enlarge the powers and responsibilities to be conferred on county district councils. The role of parish councils in focusing local opinion should if possible be strengthened.

XXII

THE WHITE PAPER ON
AREAS AND STATUS 1956

The Government rallied its feeble courage by inserting a
sentence in the White Paper stating that they 'naturally do not
take the view that no changes should be proposed to Parliament
except with the agreement of the local authorities'; but this
was immediately followed by a statement that their willing
co-operation can be of great value in carrying through any
reorganization. In consequence 'the most careful attention has
therefore been paid to the views expressed by the representatives of the Local Authority Associations'.[1] Indeed it had;
and practically no attention had been paid to anything else.
In point of fact, the Government accepted almost in their
entirety the agreed recommendations of the associations.

The basic assumption underlying the Government's conclusions is that although vast changes in the distribution of
population and industry, transportation, the scope and cost of
services and central-local relations have taken place since the
existing organization of local government was laid down
seventy-five years ago, it does not follow that radical changes
are needed. Fundamental reform could be justified only if the
present structure had shown itself incapable of meeting con-
temporary needs. That, however, is alleged not to have
occurred. 'The present system has, over many years, stood up
to the severest tests. It responded well to the abnormal demands
made on it during the war and, despite certain weaknesses, has
on the whole shown itself capable of adaptation to changing
conditions.'[2]

Just what evidence would have satisfied the Government
that the present system is incapable of meeting present-day

[1] *Areas and Status of Local Authorities in England and Wales.* Cmd. 9831/1956,
para 14.
[2] *Ibd.,* para 16.

demands is not disclosed. The long series of functions transferred to central departments or public corporations, the inability of local authorities to carry out any regional planning or development, their increasing reliance on exchequer grants, the loss of functions by county districts—these unquestionable symptoms of incapacity were passed over in silence by the White Paper in the Minister's determination to arrive at the soothing conclusion that there is 'no convincing case for radically reshaping the existing form of local government in England and Wales'.[1] All that was needed was a minor overhaul.

The rest of the White Paper spelt out in detail the Government's deferential attitude towards the associations and the desire of both the Minister and the associations to interfere to the least possible extent with vested municipal interests. The proposals follow closely on the lines agreed by the associations but with an added insistence that only very exceptional circumstances could justify any significant changes. Thus, to deprive a county borough of its independent status would be 'a most serious step which should be contemplated only where it is plainly necessary for efficient administration'.[2] Any proposal of this kind would have an added safeguard of being presented to Parliament in a separate Order, so that it could be discussed and voted on by itself. No non-county borough could be demoted to the rank of an urban district without the specific consent of the Minister, who would have to hold a public inquiry to hear any objections by the borough.[3]

The White Paper gave no lead about the best manner of dealing with the conurbations. The Government merely listed four possible methods of improving the pattern of local government in those areas of crucial importance.[4] The only points on which any divergence from the concordat was shown was in regard to the review of county districts. These would be made in the first instance by each county council; but if the Minister should consider that the proposals of a county council require radical alteration, he should be authorized to ask the Local Government Commission to carry out a review of the county districts in question and to make recommendations for their revision.[5]

[1] *Areas and Status of Local Authorities in England and Wales.* Cmd. 9831/1956, para 17.
[2] *Ibid.*, para 31.   [3] *Ibid.*, para 54.   [4] *Ibid.*, paras 38–43.   [5] *Ibid.*, para 26.

XXIII

THE LOCAL GOVERNMENT ACT, 1958

This was the background to the provisions of the Local Government Act, 1958 dealing with the reform of areas and authorities in England and Wales, and the delegation of functions to county district councils.[1] The Act broke new ground in giving the Minister a residual power to initiate changes in default of proposals made by the Commission and in excluding the metropolitan area from the jurisdiction of the Local Government Commission.[2]

The statute, like the White Paper, lays down no principles for determining the rival claims of county councils and county borough councils, which have been and still are a great source of hostility and conflict in local government. The explicit presumption that a population of 100,000 is sufficient to enable a town to discharge the responsibilities of a county borough has so far affected only the borough of Luton.[3]

The Local Government Commission is required to follow an elaborate procedure which weights the scale heavily against change. The Commission begins its review by inquiring into the prevailing conditions and consulting all the local authorities concerned, together with any other public authorities or unofficial bodies or individuals which may wish to make representations. It then prepares draft proposals which are circulated to all the authorities in the area, who may submit their objections or representations. The Commission considers these objections or representations and must confer with the local authorities concerned if they so desire. The Commission next sends a report together with its final proposals to the Minister. This also goes to all the local authorities affected, and if any of them raise an objection the Minister must order a local inquiry to be held unless he considers himself to be already fully

[1] Parts II and III, Third, Fourth and Fifth Schedules.
[2] Sections 17 and 24.   [3] Section 34.

informed on the matters to which the objection relates. The Minister's decisions are finally embodied in orders which are laid before Parliament together with the report of the Commission. The Local Government Commissions are thus only advisory bodies and the final decision rests with the Minister and Parliament. By contrast, the Local Government Boundary Commission had a direct duty of making orders which were subject to parliamentary confirmation but not to rejection or modification by the Department concerned.

The one matter in respect of which the Local Government Commission for England has a greater freedom than its predecessor is its power to recommend the institution of a 'continuous county' in a conurbation, which would involve a redistribution of functions on a novel basis.[1] This is because in a Special Review Area (the statutory term for a conurbation) it may consider functions as well as areas and the status of authorities.

The intention of the Act is that the Commission shall deal with the reorganization of the basic units of local government, namely the counties and county boroughs, leaving the county districts and the parishes to be reviewed by the county councils, although the Minister can direct the Commission to hold a review of county districts if he is dissatisfied with the proposals submitted to him by a county council, or if the latter has failed to submit any proposals.[2]

The negotiations preceding the Local Government Act, 1958, the restrictive provisions of the Act, the cumbersome procedure, and the agreement between the associations made it clear that radical reforms were unlikely to emerge from the Local Government Commission; and this has proved to be the case with one or two exceptions. The work of the Commission is, however, not yet complete, and many Ministerial decisions have still to be made.

[1] Sir William Hart: 'The Structure of Local Government' in *Local Government Today and Tomorrow*. Ed. Dudley Lofts, p. 25.
[2] Local Government Act, 1958. S. 30.

XXIV

THE WORK OF THE LOCAL GOVERNMENT COMMISSION

The most radical proposal which has so far been made by the Local Government Commission concerns the South East Lancashire Special Review Area. The Commission recommended that a continuous county be established to cover the entire conurbation together with nine most-purpose authorities making up the second tier. The new county would have a population exceeding 2,500,000 and an area approaching 500 square miles. The area at present contains more than 60 local authorities of every kind and size, ranging from Manchester County Borough (644,500 population) to a couple of parishes in the Chapel-en-le-Frith Rural District, with an estimated population of 1,400. In a very full and well-argued draft proposal the Commission explain that no other reform could hope to solve the problems facing the area. The new continuous county council would be responsible for strategic planning, major highways and traffic, police, fire protection, ambulances, civil defence, and housing (concurrently with the second tier authorities).

The nine most-purpose authorities would range from Manchester to Bury (enlarged to a population of 124,000 and an acreage of 28,800). The remaining seven have populations lying between 200,000 and 335,000. Needless to say, the County Councils of Lancashire, Cheshire, Derbyshire and the West Riding were content with the existing state of affairs, while the County Borough Councils urged the simple division of the conurbation among county boroughs.

The list of functions which the Commission desires to see conferred on the new County Council is inadequate. It does not, but should, include sewage, refuse disposal, clean air enforcement, technical education, the Ringway airport, and possibly some other activities as well.

In contrast to this resolute handling of the S.E. Lancashire situation is a feeble draft proposal for the Merseyside conurbation. Here the Special Review Area comprises a smaller population of 1,639,000. The major authorities consist of the four County Boroughs of Liverpool (745,700), Bootle (82,800), Birkenhead (141,000) and Wallasey (103,200), and the minor ones include fifteen county districts.

The Liverpool City Council was eager to see a continuous county set up to be the top tier organ for metropolitan-wide functions throughout the conurbation. The Commission rejected this obvious solution on the ground that Merseyside contains a number of county districts whose populations are well below 100,000 and it would be 'rather artificial' to amalgamate them into most-purpose authorities of reasonable size and resources. It would possibly have been difficult to give all the lower tier local authorities similar responsibilities. But would this matter? There was evidence of a fear of domination by Liverpool among the neighbouring authorities, though Liverpool's population is less than a half of that of the whole conurbation. In the end, the Commission tamely proposed a mere joint planning board for the area, adding cautiously that the board should concentrate on the smallest possible range of functions, or on a single function.

Another far-reaching proposal by the Commission was that a continuous county should be created for the Tyneside conurbation to undertake over-all functions, such as planning, overspill, large housing schemes, major highways, police, etc., while the remaining services would be performed by four boroughs.[1] These boroughs would consist of the present county boroughs of Newcastle-on-Tyne, Tynemouth, South Shields and Gateshead, to each of which would be added a number of adjacent county districts so that the enlarged boroughs would cover the entire conurbation. This plan was put forward because the Commission was impressed by the unity of the area in regard to its essential needs, the visible continuity of its development throughout the conurbation, and the similarity of its parts. The Minister has rejected the Commission's advice and proposes an all-purpose borough for the whole area (excluding Boldon).

---

[1] Local Government Commission for England. Report No. 5. Tyneside Special Review Area. July 1963.

This, he thinks, will more fully express the unity of the area.

The weakest proposals made by the Local Government Commission were those for the West Midlands Special Review Area.[1] Despite the need for a comprehensive authority to plan, co-ordinate and undertake major services throughout the Black Country, despite the clear recognition contained in its report to the Minister of the need for adequate resources and first class officers to ensure the progressive development of major services such as education, health and welfare, despite its penetrating analysis of the serious consequences resulting from obsolete boundaries, shortage of building lands, migration from county boroughs to peripheral areas, and a decline in the quality of councillors and civic leaders, the Commission shrank from any radical proposals and recommended only the replacement of the existing twenty-six local authorities of various types by five county boroughs. It rejected the idea of a comprehensive authority to plan and co-ordinate the services requiring unified treatment throughout the conurbation and proposed only a joint board to deal with the overspill, comprising representatives of Birmingham, Solihull, and the five county boroughs, and sewage disposal boards for the Thame and Upper Stour rivers. The Minister of Housing and Local Government decided against even this modest proposal for a joint overspill board. He accepted the rest of the draft report and an order to this effect has been passed by both Houses of Parliament. A positive change resulting from this report is that Solihull has become a county borough.

In the West Midlands General Review Area the Commission recommended that Burton-on-Trent, with a population of 50,000, and Worcester, with a population of 64,000, should lose their county borough status.[2] Burton-on-Trent is contesting this recommendation in the Courts.

After examining the East Midlands, the Commission concluded that the two small counties of Huntingdon and the Soke of Peterborough should be amalgamated, making a new county of only 170,000; and that the County of Cambridgeshire and

---

[1] Local Government Commission for England. Report No. 1. West Midlands Special Review Area. May 1961.

[2] *Ibid*. Report No. 2. West Midlands General Review Area. May 1961.

the Isle of Ely (also a county) be similarly required to merge.[1] These changes have been carried out. An amalgamation of all four counties would have produced a much more viable unit of nearly half a million. The proposal that the vigorous and growing motor manufacturing town of Luton be made a county borough has also been carried into effect.

The report on the West Yorkshire Special Review Area does not contemplate the creation of a continuous county for the Leeds–Bradford conurbation, but Bradford is to be slightly enlarged while Wakefield would revert to non-county borough status.[2] Dewsbury, a county borough of 53,000 population, would be combined with a number of boroughs and urban districts to make a new county borough of 165,000 persons.

In their reports on several other areas the Commission have proposed the strengthening of the stronger towns and the penalization of the weaker ones.

Thus, boundary extensions would increase the population of Derby from 132,000 to 211,000 and its rateable value from £2·1m to £2·8m; of Kingston-upon-Hull from 301,000 to 347,000 and its rateable value from £3·6m to £4·7m of Sheffield from 495,000 to 551,000 and its rateable value from £6·7m to 7·1m.[3] Middlesbrough, already a county borough of 157,000 population, would be greatly enlarged by the addition of the boroughs of Redcar and Thornaby, most of Stockton-on-Tees, the urban districts of Billingham, Eston, Saltburn and Marske-by-the-Sea, and parts of two other districts, emerging with a population of 390,000, a rateable value of £5·5m and 42,000 acres of land.[4] The proposed new county borough would extend over the main built-up area of Tees-side. The Minister has accepted the Commission's Tees-side recommendations with some modifications. He has rejected its proposals for a substantial extension of the boundaries of Nottingham.

In the South West as in the North East, boundary extensions

[1] Local Government Commission for England. Report No. 3. East Midlands General Review Area. July 1961.

[2] *Ibid*. Report No. 7. West Yorkshire Special Review Area. February 1964.

[3] *Ibid*. Report No. 8. York and North Midlands General Review Area. June 1964.

[4] *Ibid*. Report No. 6. North Eastern General Review Area. October 1963.

are recommended for the more important towns, such as Bath, Bristol, Exeter and Gloucester.[1] Gloucester, with a population even when its boundaries are extended of only 85,000, will remain a county borough, while Cheltenham, with a population of 90,000 when enlarged, is refused county borough status by the Minister.

In East Anglia the Commission recommended substantial extensions of Grimsby and Norwich, which would increase the populations of these county boroughs from 95,000 to 130,000 in the former case, and from 119,000 to 161,000 in the latter. Great Yarmouth, whose population is only 52,000, would lose its county borough status and become a non-county borough in Norfolk. Lincolnshire is at present divided into three administrative counties. The Commission proposed that two of them (Holland and Kesteven) should be amalgamated to make a larger county of 237,000 population. The third county in Lincolnshire (Lindsey) would lose about ten per cent of its present population of 348,500.[2]

[1] Local Government Commission for England. Report No. 4. South Western General Review Area. January 1963.
[2] *Ibid.* Report No. 9. Lincolnshire and East Anglia General Review Area.

XXV

THE CASE OF RUTLAND

Another proposal for the East Midlands was that Rutland should be absorbed by Leicestershire. As every schoolboy knows, Rutland with a mere 25,000 population is England's smallest county, and its survival as a separate administrative county has for long been regarded as the classic example of the obsolete character of our present structure. Rutland is sparsely populated throughout; it has only two small towns, Oakham (4,200) and Uppingham (1,900); and people go to Leicester when they need to use a major shopping or service centre.

In local government it is highly dependent on its neighbours. Other local education authorities provide all the grammar school places and nearly all the further education for Rutland's pupils, specialist advice about education, the youth employment service, and facilities for handicapped children. A similar position exists in the health and welfare services. The Rutland County Council obtains from other local authorities all the reception and residential accommodation it needs for its children other than foster homes; nearly all the facilities required for the blind, deaf and physically handicapped, and almost all the mental health service. It leans on the Leicestershire County Council for the fire service and for its library books. Its police force was taken away in 1951. Thus Rutland is little more than a purchaser of municipal services provided by other local authorities.

The Local Government Commission observed that this is not really local government at all, and recommended that Rutland be merged with Leicestershire. The Rutland County Council than began an intensive campaign to persuade the Government to reject the obviously sensible advice they had received. The council projected its image as that of David fighting Goliath, of John Hampden resisting the payment of ship-money, of Jack the Giant-killer fearlessly fighting the forces of bureaucracy, bigness, tidiness, rationality, logic, take-over bids, large-scale enterprise, modernization—in fact all the things most disliked by the British people. Sir Keith Joseph, the Tory Minister of Housing and Local Government, succumbed to these absurd blandishments, and so—presumably on the principle *de minimis lex non curat*—Rutland survives, neither bloody nor bowed.

XXVI

THE UPSURGE OF THE COUNTIES

Increases in the number of county boroughs or the enlargement of their boundaries can only be made at the expense of the counties in which they are located. This, of course, is the reason for the bitter conflict which has existed between county and county borough councils for the past forty years. The spokesmen for the county councils give the impression that the counties have been severely injured by the growth and expansion of county boroughs. The falsity of this has been proved by the Local Government Commission, which pointed out that whereas between 1921 and 1931 the population of counties and county boroughs increased at approximately the same rate. From 1931 to 1951 the population of the counties grew six times as fast; while since 1951 the whole increase of population has occurred in the county areas. In 1921 the counties had 58 per cent of the population in England and the county boroughs 42 per cent. Today, the county share has risen to 65 per cent and the county borough share has fallen to 35 per cent. If London be excluded, the swing in favour of the counties is even greater. The reason is, of course, that the growth of urban population has occurred in the suburbs of great cities lying outside their administrative boundaries.

I have indicated the major changes so far proposed by the Local Government Commission for England without knowing how far the Minister will accept, reject or modify several of them. They must, moreover, be passed by both Houses of Parliament. I have not attempted an exhaustive account of the Commission's proposals but have stressed the main trends. It may be assumed, however, that these indicate the general dimensions of probable change although the Commission's proposals for several important areas have not yet been published; and on that assumption it is clear that reform is likely

119

LOCAL GOVERNMENT IN CRISIS

to take place only on a modest scale. As Sir William Hart has remarked, 'the local government system had developed a built-in rigidity resistant to change',[1] and the predictable result of the Minister's consultations with the associations in 1955 is 'no grand measure of reform of local government, but at most a restricted reorganization'.[2] The responsibility for this rests more on the local authorities, the local authority associations and the Ministry of Housing and Local Government than on the Local Government Commission, though the latter has frequently displayed a lack of boldness and imagination, as in the case of its failure to grapple firmly with the problem of the conurbations except in the South East Lancashire and Tyneside areas.

[1] 'The Structure of Local Government' in *Local Government Today and Tomorrow*. (Ed. Dudley Lofts), p. 22.
[2] *Op cit.*, p. 23.

XXVII

THE SITUATION IN WALES

The Local Government Commission for Wales was faced with a much harder task owing to the fact that all possibility of one or more Special Review Areas for Wales was omitted due to pressure brought by Welsh M.P.s when the Local Government Act, 1958 was before the Standing Committee of the House of Commons. The Local Government Commission for Wales expressed regret at its inability to apply for the whole or part of Wales to be made a Special Review Area. It found Wales to be overgoverned at the local level[1] and undergoverned at the regional level.

A good idea of the attitude of Welsh local authorities to reform can be obtained from the Commission's report.[2] When it entered on its task there were thirteen counties with populations ranging from 18,000 in Radnorshire to three-quarters of a million in Glamorganshire. Seven of them have less than 100,000 each, and six have less than 60,000. Rateable resources are low and rates are high. Indeed, all the ten local authorities which levied rates in excess of 30s. 0d. in the £ were in Wales. With the exception of Flintshire all the counties receive Rate Deficiency Grants at a higher percentage than the average for county councils in England and Wales.

The Commission formed three main conclusions: (1) That several of the counties are too small in population and with insufficient resources to provide a satisfactory standard of services. Larger counties are therefore needed. (2) In forming the larger units, the poorer and more sparsely populated areas of mid-Wales should be associated with the more prosperous

---

[1] Radnorshire, for example, with a population of 18,000, has a county council, three urban district councils, five rural district councils, twenty-two parish councils and many parish meetings—a total of thirty-one councils.
[2] Local Government Commission for Wales. Report and Proposals for Wales. December 1962.

industrialized parts of the county. (3) That to propitiate public sentiment and local patriotism the amalgamation of whole counties should take place.

These three conclusions were rejected out of hand by the representatives of the county councils who appeared before the Commission. The wealthy opposed the idea of helping the needy. The poor rejected the notion that they need help. Everyone denied that the small size of the counties is an obstacle to effective local government; and in any case they opposed the conception that administrative efficiency should be the dominant criterion. Much fuss was made over the difficulty of travelling long distances to council meetings. The incompatibility of outlook and interest among people living in different parts of the country was emphasized as a disadvantage in amalgamating some of the smaller units. The Local Government Commission for Wales was in effect invited, in its own words, 'to fossilize existing situations'. The old and inadequate remedy of joint action was put forward as the remedy for all ills. The Commission disagreed with nearly all the special pleading of the witnesses who appeared before it, and was clearly sceptical of many of the arguments put forward. But the sheer weight of opposition, which it suspected was the result of a gentleman's agreement among the local authorities concerned, led it to modify its original proposals. Instead of the four large counties it had at first conceived as the pattern of a reorganized structure it recommended seven counties together with three county boroughs (Cardiff, Newport and Swansea), with Merthyr Tydvil reverting to non-county borough status.

XXVIII

THE LIBERAL PARTY'S SCHEME
FOR WALES 1962

A much bolder and more imaginative proposal was put forward by the Liberal Party.[1] This advocates a directly elected Council for Wales to take over from the county and county borough councils large-scale services such as the police, further education, fire services, water supply, main roads, special schools and planning. The Council could also be entrusted with several functions at present carried out by the Central Government or public corporations, such as trunk roads, economic development, public transport, hospitals, control over the location of industry and offices. Subject to these changes the administrative counties could continue in their present form. They could administer primary and secondary education, health services, children's and old persons' homes, planning control, etc. Merthyr Tydvil could remain a county borough. The rural district councils and the smaller urban districts would be abolished, leaving only the town councils and the parish councils—the latter being reconstructed as valley councils.

The Local Government Commission was precluded by the terms of the Act from even considering such a sane and sensible proposition as this. All it could do was to point out the need to consider not only areas and authorities but other relevant matters as well. 'Indeed', it reported, *'when next the local government of Wales comes to be reviewed,* the inquiry should in our opinion be directed not only to boundaries but to functions, to the financial system of rates and grants, and to the constituent units and their relation to one another. . . . So comprehensive a review may well entail a radical remodelling of the structure

---

[1] *Local Government.* A Report to the Liberal Party (May 1962). Liberal Publications Department. See also Alderman Edgar L. Chappell: *The Government of Wales* (Foyles, 1943) for an excellent discussion.

of local government.'[1] Could anything be more absurd than to appoint an intelligent group of persons to examine the local government situation, but hamstringing them so as to preclude their putting forward the changes they think desirable? Pusillanimity and conservatism could scarcely go further.

However, the Government has apparently taken a deep breath and is having second and perhaps third thoughts about the matter.

[1] My italics.

XXIX

THE PRINCIPAL DEFECTS
OF THE STRUCTURE

There are three principal defects in the structure as it at present exists. One is that there are many authorities in all categories which are too small in terms of area, rateable value or population to provide an adequate base for existing municipal services. We may hope—despite the survival of Rutland—that some of these will disappear by amalgamation as a result of the reviews of major authorities by the Local Government Commission and the review of county districts by county councils which will follow.

A second defect is that the structure has engendered a bitter conflict between county councils and county borough councils which has been gnawing at the vitals of local government for the past forty years. This has absorbed the time and energies of councillors, councils, and local government associations which could have been better spent in constructive tasks and has diverted their attention from the real problems facing them. The conflict arises from the strong desire of large and growing towns to acquire county borough status, and of county borough councils to extend their boundaries, and the equally strong desire of the county councils to resist these changes at all costs.

It is easy to see how the conflict has arisen. As a city grows its suburbs extend beyond the borough boundaries; outlying villages or housing estates coalesce with the expanding urban area, and more and more people move out from the county borough to these more attractive residential settlements, while continuing to work in the city. The county boroughs naturally wish to extend their boundaries to encompass these residential settlements; they regard this expansion as a normal feature of town growth, and they resent and deplore the widespread decline in population of the densely built-up cities. Moreover, they are often in great need of land for rehousing their poorer inhabitants at a better standard.

The case for the county boroughs seems reasonable until we look at the matter from the standpoint of the counties. The county councils have been asked to accept new responsibilities in the spheres of education, police, planning, fire brigades and health services. How can they perform these tasks in a proper manner if they are liable to lose the wealthiest and most populous parts of their territories? The Scott Committee[1] rightly urged the need to raise the standard of local government services in the rural areas so as to give the countryman and his children an equal opportunity with the town dweller. How could the counties provide improved services if they were to be left with only straggling, sparse-populated areas of low rateable value?

The truth of the matter is that the administrative dichotomy embodied in the Local Government Act, 1888, which introduced the distinction between county council and county borough, is an outworn conception. The trends of physical development, the pattern of social and economic life, and the spread of motor transport all point towards the closer integration of town and country life.

The situation which confronts us calls for a much more marked degree of physical separation between town and country than has prevailed during recent decades; indeed, planners are agreed upon the need to re-establish the age-long distinction between urban and rural communities which has become blurred and even obliterated as a result of sporadic building and uncontrolled development. At the same time there is need for a much greater integration of town and country for administrative and financial purposes of common interest.

This conflict can be overcome only by merging county and county borough councils in larger organs which transcend their particular interests. Such a merging is possible, within the terms of reference of the Local Government Commission, only in the Special Review Areas, apart from Greater London, to which I will refer later. The 'merging' consists in creating what is called a continuous county extending over the whole

[1] Report of the Committee on Land Utilization in Rural Areas (1942), p. 159.

conurbation. This super-county would exercise those functions calling for unified handling throughout the area, such as strategic planning, main roads, traffic control, technical education, water supply, sewage, refuse disposal, overspill housing, police and fire services. The county boroughs—which would become nominally county districts—would remain in command of many services not usually administered by non-county boroughs or urban districts. They would, in fact, become most-purpose authorities but would be brought back into the county for certain overriding purposes. Much of the venom and bitterness would be taken out of the city-versus-county struggle if county boroughs ceased to be independent in all respects of the counties in which they are situated, even though they would continued to enjoy a large measure of autonomy.

The third defect is that the present structure does not provide for effective performance of services requiring large areas of administration or planning, or both. In consequence, functions requiring regional planning or administration cannot be entrusted to local authorities but must be performed by *ad hoc* bodies, Government Departments, or authorities appointed by Ministers.

The Local Government Act, 1958 defined Special Review Areas for Tyneside, West Yorkshire, South East Lancashire, Merseyside and West Midlands. It may be asked: do not these Special Review Areas present opportunities for creating just the kind of directly-elected regional councils which I advocate? Unfortunately they do not. The Special Review Areas were defined by the Local Government Act, 1958 to comprise only the built-up parts of the conurbations without including any rural or semi-rural hinterland. The statute makes no attempt to deal with the regional problem, which extends far beyond the built-up limits of the conurbations. The Act does, however, permit the Commission to ask the Minister to vary the area of a scheduled conurbation. The Local Government Commission asked the Minister to extend the Manchester and Merseyside Special Review Areas so as to close the gap between them. Several local authorities opposed this and in July 1964 the Minister asked the Commission to hold further talks with them. After doing so the Commission repeated its request, the effect of which would have been to cause the eastern boundary of Merseyside to coincide with the western boundary of Manchester. This request was refused by the Minister and this caused Professor Ely Devons to resign from the Commission.

What is now known as the city region is one of the most important phenomena of our age. It is the outcome of the scientific and technological advances which have given us improved methods of transport and communication, enabling people to live further and further away from their work, and thus for urban man to spread out his places of work, residence and recreation throughout an ever-widening territory. Yet the core city remains the focal centre of the complex, which may contain many sub-centres of various kinds, together with satellite towns, housing estates, self-contained suburbs and so forth.

XXX

DEMOCRATIC REGIONAL GOVERNMENT

The most desirable reform would be the creation both in the city regions and in the conurbations of directly-elected regional councils covering the industrial, commercial and residential core and also a wide stretch of rural and semi-rural hinterland, extending far beyond the suburbs and comprising domitory settlements, outlying villages and farms, a green belt or a brown agricultural belt, garden cities or smaller towns and so forth. These regional councils would be responsible for regional planning and the administration of services requiring large-scale administration, such as the larger housing projects, main drainage and sewage disposal, main highways and bridges, water supply, the provision of large parks and open spaces, the disposal of refuse, civil airfields, river conservancy and flood prevention, technical education, passenger road services, etc.,

In order to establish general regional councils of this kind it will be necessary to compromise between the needs of the various services in the determination of appropriate areas. This may involve the sacrifice of perfection in some spheres of activity, but although all boundaries present some anomalies, it is possible to delimit areas which will broadly satisfy the main regional needs. The alternatives to a solution of this kind are so calamitous to local government that we must not allow action to be impeded by the technical difficulty of defining suitable regions.[1]

Below the regional council there will be a second tier of municipal authorities administering the local services in urban or rural areas respectively within the region. The regions will be too large to be administered by a single authority and a

[1] A useful discussion of the regional problem is contained in three recent publications of the Acton Society Trust. They are entitled *Regional Institutions— a guide*; *Regionalism in England; its Natures and Purpose 1905–65*; and *Regionalism; The New Regional Machinery*.

double-deck system will therefore be required. The principle of major and minor authorities which is embodied in county government would thus be preserved and projected on a larger scale. It would be applied to the conurbations which, apart from London, are largely administered by county borough councils. The conception of a two-tier system for the great conurbation, the city region or the metropolitan area is right in principle.

The case for projecting local government on to a regional scale is gaining wide support among persons of all political views who have given serious thought to the matter.

Mr Derek Senior has recently made an eloquent plea for making the city region the basis for a reorganized system of local government.[1] He emphasises two points. One is that the city region is an established fact, although it has not been recognized for administrative purposes. The other is that the city region must be distinguished from the much larger regions which are used for central government purposes, and which he thinks should properly be called provinces.

A city region in Mr Senior's sense is different from a conurbation, just as Greater London cannot be accurately described as a conurbation. He is undoubtedly right in stressing the futility in the present age of considering large towns as separate entities divorced from the surrounding countryside, peri-urban areas, suburbs, villages, housing estates, etc. Where his analysis will command less agreement is in the delineation of his thirty-odd city regions; but that aspect of his scheme could be modified without jeopardizing the basic principles. His proposal envisages a two-tier structure designed to give a large measure of independence in matters of purely local concern to the well-developed communities often found on the outskirts of large cities.

Two schemes which place their main emphasis on democratic regionalism have recently emerged from two associations of young conservatives, namely the Young Conservative Policy Group and the Bow Group.

The former group proposes the abolition of all the existing local authorities and their replacement by a new two-tier

[1] 'The City Region as an Administrative Unit'. 36 *Political Quarterly*, p. 82 (January–March 1965).

structure. The top tier would consist of seventeen directly elected Regional Councils (twelve for England, three for Scotland and two for Wales) to be the overall authorities for planning and economic development. They would also be responsible for overall transport co-ordination, major road construction, regional police, fire brigades, civil defence, the ambulance service, conservation and planning of water supply, and they would also be able to pass local private Bills. The second tier would comprise district councils which would carry out all the other functions of local government, including education, health and housing. The largest units would be existing cities but even the smallest ones would be at least as large as a parliamentary constituency, and sometimes two or three constituencies.[1]

The Young Conservative scheme has not been worked out and is presented only in the barest outline. It has severe defects in respect of the regional divisions and the allocation of functions between the two tiers; but it has the great merit of boldness and imagination.

The Bow Group advocates at least eight regions, to be established in Northern England, the East and West Pennines, Wales, the Midlands, East Anglia, the South West and South East (there would be sub-regions for Greater London, North Thames and South Thames). These would be very large areas, with populations ranging from 2m to 16m.[2]

The Bow Group is anxious to decentralize government, but only to democratic bodies. It wants the people of the regions to be able to exert a greater influence on national economic and social policies than they have been able to do in the past or than is possible through the appointed Regional Advisory Councils set up by the Labour Government. The scheme therefore proposes directly-elected regional councils. The number of members would depend on the population of each region, but the general idea is that the ratio of councillors to voters would be similar to that prevailing in parliamentary representation.

[1] *Blueprint for Britain.* Report by the Young Conservatives on the Reconstruction of Britain. C.P.C. No. 310. May 1965.
[2] *New Life for Local Government.* Published by the Conservative Political Centre.

The average regional council would have about seventy members, of which a certain proportion (seven to fifteen) would be full-time councillors. These full-time councillors would form a regional cabinet (to be called an Executive Board). The Chairman of the Executive Board would be chosen by the majority party and he would select the other members. The Chairman would receive a salary of £5,000 p.a. and the other full-time members £4,000 p.a. Part-time regional councillors would be paid £1,000 p.a. and an attendance fee of £3 for each committee meeting. The cabinet system would be introduced.

The Bow Group's regional councils would be responsible for economic and environmental planning and for overall development control; for education policy and the actual administration of further and technical education; police; fire and ambulance services; hospitals; main drainage; highways and traffic managment; bus services; central libraries and the co-ordination of district libraries; the design of schools and houses; entertainments and cultural services; refuse disposal; and a research and intelligence service.

Each region would be divided into regional districts with a minimum population of 100,000 and a maximum of 500,000. These would have directly-elected councils whose powers would comprise housing management, planning control, health and welfare, children's services and the other functions usually regarded as appropriate to district authorities.

Villages and small towns possessing a strong sense of identity would be allowed to carry out a few minor functions through community councils. Examples of their activities are local entertainments, the appointment of school governors and the letting of council houses.

In a recent Fabian tract[1] Mr L. J. Sharpe explains the need for larger units of local government; he urges that the new enlarged counties should wherever possible be based on the boundaries of city regions, but he observes that city regions do not exist in all parts of the country, so Mr Senior's solution could not apply everywhere. Finally, he urges that the conurbations should be widened to include their hinterlands.

[1] *Why Local Democracy?* by L. J. Sharpe. Fabian Tract 361.

All of these recent writings on local government draw attention to the need for much larger authorities covering regional areas; all of them favour a two-tier system in all or most of such areas; and all of them imply that the powers of the Local Government Commission are insufficient to produce the kind of structure which is required.

There are, however, significant differences in the several approaches. Mr Senior and Mr Sharpe appear to accept regional (or provincial) administration and planning as an emanation of the central government, whereas the Young Conservative Groups seek to replace it forthwith by democratically elected regional organs. Moreover, both the Bow Group and the Young Conservatives contemplate much larger regions than Mr Senior's city regions or Mr Sharpe's expanded conurbations. The independent county borough survives as a single tier authority only in Mr Sharpe's plea for 'the really larger towns'.[1]

If regional councils were established there would be a practicable alternative to the transfer of functions from local authorities to central departments or special bodies. After all, the hospitals were nationalized in order to be regionalized. Unless a bold step of this kind is taken, we may well repeat the mistake which was made in the nineteenth century of creating a series of separate bodies for individual services; boards of guardians, health boards, school boards, improvement commissioners, highway boards and several others. This is certain to lead to confusion, extravagence and inefficiency.

One feature which emerges with monotonous regularity is the opposition of almost all local authorities, whatever their size and rank, to any structural changes except those which would enlarge their individual areas or raise their own status.

The slow processes of reorganization now taking place in England and Wales have been aptly described by Sir William Hart as 'the scanty fruits of much talk of the reform of local government: a modest measure of reorganization, far from fundamental in intention or effect. The framework and machinery established in the latter part of the nineteenth century remains largely intact: certainly it does not show any substantial change

[1] *Op. cit.*, p. 24.

of external appearance.'[1] I entirely share Sir William's belief that if the problems of today, such as those presented by motor cars, urban renewal and overspill, are to be solved by local government, far more drastic reforms than any so far attempted will be necessary. He envisages a regional structure with elected salaried representatives, a cabinet system and greater discretion given to officers.[2]

The present reforms are the outcome of discussions which aimed at achieving the minimum changes needed to prevent a breakdown. They involved horse trading, compromise and concessions at every stage; they have resulted in the devising of procedures which weight the scale heavily against change; they have been marked by a lack of courage on the part of the Government and a lack of vision on the part of the local authorities and their associations. It is a story of pusillanimity and procrastination.

---

[1] Sir William Hart: 'The Structure of Local Government' in *Local Government Today and Tomorrow*. Ed. Dudley Lofts, p. 25.

[2] See his address to the annual conference of the Institute of Municipal Treasurers and Accountants. *The Times*, June 11, 1965.

XXXI

THE REFORM OF LONDON GOVERNMENT

The story of the London government reforms present a refreshing contrast, although it had a most unpromising start.

London was excluded from the jurisdiction of the ill-fated Local Government Boundary Commission in 1945; and the appointment of the short-lived Reading Committee was merely absurd. The White Paper of 1956 on *Areas and Status of Local Authorities* followed the precedent by saying that none of the proposals it contained applied to the County of London. Moreover, the County of Middlesex was to retain its two-tier system and none of its large non-county boroughs were to achieve county borough status. The remaining parts of the metropolitan area, the White Paper declared, were to be considered on similar lines to the other conurbations and would accordingly be included within the jurisdiction of the Local Government Commission for England, which in the course of its review would be bound to consider whether any matters should and could be handled 'jointly on behalf of Greater London as a whole'.[1] If so, it could make whatever recommendations it thought desirable to attain that end. The word 'jointly' was significant.

Fortunately, this plan was never carried out. It would have left the LCC and the Middlesex County Council intact, and would have defeated any hope of achieving a truly metropolitan government for Greater London. One would like to know just what happened inside the Ministry of Housing and Local Government when Mr Henry Brooke, who had long experience and great knowledge of London government, succeeded Mr Duncan Sandys as Minister of Housing and Local Government in January 1957. All that is publicly known is that when the

[1] Paras 45–46.

Local Government Bill appeared in 1957 the Metropolitan Area was defined in a separate schedule apart from the five conurbations and was excluded from the areas to be reviewed by the Local Government Commission. Instead, a Royal Commission was appointed to inquire into the local government of Greater London.

The reform of London was long overdue. The LCC was given the same area as that assigned to its predecessor, the Metropolitan Board of Works, in 1855. This area had no relation to the size and spread of London even in 1889 when the County of London was created. The lack of a metropolitan authority extending over a wider area led inevitably, in London as elsewhere, to the creation of a number of *ad hoc* bodies such as the Metropolitan Police Commission, the Metropolitan Water Board, the Port of London Authority, the London Passenger Transport Board (now known as London Transport) and later additions for gas, electricity, hospitals and other services.

I demonstrated the need for reform as long ago as 1939 in my book *The Government and Misgovernment of London*. No official attempt was made to inquire into the matter until the appointment of the Royal Commission in 1957. This was the first occasion when the system of local government in the metropolitan area was examined as a whole to see what changes, if any, would bring about more effective and convenient local government.

The strength of the Royal Commission lay in the high calibre of its members and the fact that none of them represented vested municipal interests. The chairman, Sir Edwin Herbert (now Lord Tangley), is an eminent lawyer with a distinguished record of public service. He has never taken part in local government. Mr Paul Cadbury lives and works in Birmingham, Professor W. J. M. Mackenzie occupies the Chair of Government in Manchester University and Sir Charles Morris was Vice-Chancellor of Leeds University. Miss Johnson is Deputy Chairman of the National Assistance Board, Sir John Wrigley is a former deputy secretary of the Ministry of Housing and Local Government with a special knowledge of housing, and Mr William Lawson is a former president of the Institute of Chartered Accountants and a member of the Southern Electricity Board.

The high quality of the report reflects the calibre of the Royal Commission. It is lucid, coherent, well written and well arranged. It looks backwards to the past and forward to the future. It keeps one eye firmly fixed on administrative efficiency, and the other no less firmly fixed on the health of democratic local government. Its unanimous recommendations aim at improving the position in both respects. These are the qualities which made the report a great state document.

The weaknesses of the report were mostly due to circumstances beyond the Commission's control. Thus, the 'review area' was far too restricted: it covered only the built-up portion of Greater London with a slight incursion into the green belt. All the *ad hoc* bodies were expressly excluded from the Commission's terms of reference. (It was subsequently announced, however, that the Metropolitan Water Board will be abolished and its functions transferred to the Greater London Council.)

The Herbert report described in detail the defects of the structure in terms of the shortcomings of the principal municipal services. The Commission outlined four possible methods of overcoming the existing difficulties. They were: (1) For the central government to take over some of the functions requiring unified treatment for the whole metropolis. This would involve not one Department but many, and a big problem of co-ordination would arise. (2) The creation of more single-purpose bodies to deal with particular functions. The drawbacks of *ad hockery*, as I call it, are that the public corporations or other organs concerned are not elected or politically responsible in the way that a municipal council is; as one-purpose bodies they are required to concentrate attention on a single function irrespective of its effect on related functions, so that co-ordination is often conspicuous by its absence; and the fabric of local government is weakened by the removal of important services from its sphere of activities. (3) Joint boards or committees composed of existing units. This is a solution which has been tried in many places and has seldom if ever succeeded. (4) A local authority of wider scope than any hitherto existing.

In a challenging passage the report declared 'the choice before local government in Greater London is, in truth, to abdicate in favour of central government, or to reform so as to be equipped to deal with present-day problems'.[1] The Commission came down firmly on the side of reform.

And so, too, did the Macmillan Government, to its credit. It accepted the basic recommendations of the report, subject to modifications in two respects. One of these concerned the size and number of London Boroughs. The other concerned the method of administering education.

The reorganization of local government in the metropolis is founded on two major propositions. First, that a directly elected council should be set up to undertake functions which need to be planned or administered by a single body for the entire metropolis. Second, that everything else can be entrusted to a separately elected tier of local authorities.

Thus we now have the Greater London Council presiding over an area containing a resident population of almost 8m and extending over 620 square miles. It has a rateable value of £607m. The former County of London had a population of 3·2m, an area of 117 square miles and a rateable value of £110m. Greater London has a greater population than any one of ten European nations, including Austria, Bulgaria, Switzerland, Sweden and Norway.

In the review area there were formerly some 118 local authorities. They consisted of the LCC, Middlesex County Council, parts of Kent, Essex, Hertfordshire and Surrey County Councils, three county borough councils, the City of London Corporation, twenty-eight Metropolitan borough councils, forty-three non-county boroughs, twenty-eight urban district councils, three rural district councils and six parish councils. This medley has been swept away[2] and replaced by the Greater London Council and thirty-two London borough councils, plus the ancient City.

The Herbert report advised provisionally that there should be fifty-two boroughs with populations of between 100,000 and 150,000. The Government considered that the London boroughs should be larger than that, and after careful inquiries carried

[1] Report of Royal Commission on Local Government in Greater London, Cmnd 1164/1960. H.M.S.O., para 707.
[2] So far as Greater London is concerned; but not all the review area is included therein.

out by four town clerks decided on thirty-two boroughs in Greater London. Their average population is about 250,000. Their actual population ranges from 146,000 in Kingston-upon-Thames to 340,000 in Lambeth. Their areas range from Bromley with nearly 40,000 acres to Kensington and Chelsea with only 2,951; their densities from 7·5 to the acre in Bromley to 74 to the acre in Kensington and Chelsea; and their rateable value from £97m in Westminster to less than £9m in Sutton. Despite these unavoidable variations, the London boroughs are a much stronger, larger and richer group of local authorities than those they have replaced. An essential feature of the reform was to bring into existence a second tier on which much larger responsibilities could safely be devolved. I think the Government's policy was an improvement on the Herbert Commission's proposals.

The main functions assigned to the Greater London Council are the strategic planning of the whole Metropolis; major schemes of comprehensive development, such as those on the South Bank, the Elephant and Castle, Knightsbridge, etc.; metropolitan roads, which comprise about 500 miles of bus routes; traffic regulation throughout the Metropolis; the fire service; refuse disposal; ambulances; the sewage system; building regulation; the licensing of petrol filling stations, theatres, cinemas and betting tracks; parks and open spaces used by Londoners generally such as Kenwood, the Crystal Palace and Hampstead Heath; entertainments, concerts and museums of more than purely local interest, such as the Royal Festival Hall; and a research and information service. In the sphere of housing, the Greater London Council is in sole charge of overspill housing outside Greater London; for expanding towns under the Town Development Act; for housing and slum clearance *inside* the conurbation if either the London borough council concerned agrees or the Minister of Housing and Local Government gives his consent. The GLC has inherited nearly 250,000 dwellings from the LCC.[1]

The borough councils are housing authorities within their respective areas; they will do the detailed planning of those

---

[1] The G.L.C. has the ownership and control of these dwellings until such time as the Minister of Housing and Local Government may otherwise determine.

areas in conformity with the strategic overall plan made by the Greater London Council and approved by the Minister; they are in charge of planning control functions; they are responsible for the construction, repair, lighting and cleansing of all roads other than metropolitan roads and trunk roads (if the Minister of Transport decides to have any of the latter within the metropolitan region). They have taken over from the county councils the personal health services, welfare services and the children services—a new and important task elsewhere performed by county borough and county councils. In this sphere they must provide accommodation and welfare services for old and disabled persons, look after the homeless, the widows, the unmarried mothers, the blind and the handicapped, and take care of deprived children. They are responsible for supervising adoption, administering remand homes, and providing facilities for mental patients transferred from hospitals to 'community care'. They provide and maintain public libraries, swimming pools, baths and washhouses, cemeteries and crematoria, local parks, open spaces and recreation grounds. They collect the garbage (but do not dispose of it). They are the rating authorities and the GLC precepts on them for its own needs. They carry out a large number of regulatory services in respect of such matters as food and drugs, markets, shops, animals, clean air, explosives, weights and measures, and riding schools.

Education was the one major topic on which the Herbert Commission failed to formulate a clear and persuasive policy. The report proposed a division of functions between the GLC and the borough councils which was confused and unconvincing. The position was in any event one of exceptional difficulty because in the County of London the LCC was the local education authority, without any functions being exercised by the metropolitan borough councils, whereas in the other parts of Greater London education functions were either delegated to divisional executives or excepted districts, or in West Ham, East Ham and Croydon centred in the county borough council.

The Government originally intended to make the London borough councils local education authorities throughout the metropolis; but protests by teachers and parents at the prospective break-up of the unified education service the LCC had built up, and the lack of any experience in this sphere by the metropolitan boroughs, led the Government to adopt a compromise. In the former County of London a body known as the Inner London Education Authority has been set up. This is legally a Committee of the GLC; it consists of the elected members of the GLC for inner London together with a representative nominated by each of the twelve inner London borough councils. The rateborne expenditure of the ILEA will fall entirely on the inner London boroughs.

In the rest of Greater London each London borough council is responsible for education as an independent local education authority.

This, briefly, is the essence of the London reforms. They are fundamentally a projection on a larger scale of the system which had existed for more than sixty years in the County of London, but with a considerable redistribution of functions.

The London Government Act, 1963, is not a perfect measure. It contains errors of omission and of commission. Thus, the ancient corporation of the City of London has once again escaped the winds of change that have blown over the metropolis, and this is both inexcusable and deplorable. The larger regional problem has been left untouched. The GLC has been treated as just another local authority, as regards the number of its members, unpaid councillors and aldermen, and reliance on the Committee system, though its sheer size raises doubts as to the efficacy of these traditional features. Unquestionably the members of the Greater London Council should be paid; and at least the chairmen of committees should receive substantial salaries. The election of aldermen should have been discontinued. The GLC should have been given greater powers in regard to planning control, housing and highways. I can see no reason why trunk routes under the direct control of the Minister of Transport should exist in Greater London, and the Minister's powers over traffic regulation and highways generally are excessive. In the sphere of planning it would have been preferable to give planning control powers to the GLC and allow them to delegate such powers on a generous scale to the boroughs. Of greater importance is the failure to give the GLC exclusive control of the planning and development of the central area—the small but supremely important heart of the great metropolis which contains almost all the institutions, monuments, buildings and landmarks which give London its significance as a national capital and a great intermational centre.[1] The planning and development of this heart is at present divided among no fewer than nine of the new London borough councils. How can one hope for a worthwhile development of this central area under such conditions? In regard to housing, the GLC should have concurrent powers with the borough councils to provide houses anywhere in the metropolis, without having to obtain the agreement of the borough council or the approval of the Minister.

Finally, no attempt has been made to integrate the *ad hoc* authorities with the new Greater London Council, or even to provide a formal link between the GLC on the one hand and the public transport authorities on the other.

Despite these shortcomings—and one could add further criticisms—everyone who cares for local government or who understands the problems of metropolitan government must rejoice at the London reforms. The basic features of the new structure are right in principle. At last we have a Greater London authority which can look with a single eye at the entire metropolis in regard to such essential services as strategic planning, main highways and traffic regulation, housing and overspill, fire services and refuse disposal, sewage and the ambulance service.

The Greater London system is in the authentic tradition of local self-government. It avoids an extension of *ad hockery*, and its concomitant disadvantages to which I have already drawn attention. It also avoids the futility and procrastination of joint committees or boards. It offers a promise of high achievement for the future; and one may reasonably expect that, if the GLC exercises its present somewhat limited functions in such a way as to gain public support and confidence, its powers will in due course be enlarged in scope and depth.

The future of the London borough councils will similarly depend on how well they do their job and whether they make

[1] See W. A. Robson: *The Heart of Greater London*; Greater London Paper published by the London School of Economics and Political Science.

a conscious effort to enhance the spirit of citizenship and a sense of community among their citizens. This is the ultimate test of success. Civic greatness is not to be identified with mere size. It is to be seen rather in the quality of the environment both physical and spiritual: the degree to which a city (whether great or small) expresses health, beauty and convenience and thus makes possible the good life.

The Herbert Commission received almost no help from most of the local authorities in Greater London. All of them (except three metropolitan borough councils) gave written evidence; and the great majority attended the public sittings and made oral representations. But the evidence convinced the Herbert commission that 'notwithstanding the many virtues of local government today the parochial outlook that has been one of the great obstacles to any serious reform of London government is still very much alive'.[1] Many of the views expressed on behalf of local authorities were based on emotional rather than rational considerations and were of little use to the Royal Commission. With only half-a-dozen exceptions out of more than a hundred local government bodies, 'no local authority seemed prepared to recognize that there was a case for the exercise of wide powers over the review area as a whole, or indeed the existence of any pressing problems which needed common consideration'.[2] The London County Council was particularly unco-operative and refused to recognize that there were any problems needing attention in the metropolis, or even that there was any need for a Royal Commission or central government intervention. It stubbornly insisted that 'London' was synonymous with the County of London. It would not permit their chief officers to give evidence or to appear as witnesses before the commission.

The recommendations of the Herbert report, the proposals of the Government and the London Government Bill were met with unrelenting opposition on the part of a majority of the local authorities concerned, regardless of size, status or political complexion; by the Standing Joint Committee of Metropolitan Borough Councils; and by many of the professional bodies concerned with local government. The London Labour Party

[1] Report, p. 43. [2] Ibid., p. 44.

143

denounced the Bill as a Tory plot to destroy the Labour hold on the LCC, where it had been in power for more than thirty years. The Parliamentary Labour Party opposed it in each House clause by clause, sentence by sentence, almost word by word. The doctors, the teachers, the architects, the social workers and the magistrates of juvenile courts all sorrowfully declared that the great achievements which had resulted from long years of effort by the London County Council and other county councils would be sacrified by the threatened reforms, which they regarded as unnecessary and harmful.

These reactions are typical of the attitudes of local authorities and their staffs towards reorganization. Similar attitudes can be found in many other countries of the Western World, and particularly in the USA. They reflect prevailing attitudes among local authorities in the rest of England and Wales, as the Local Government Commission has found to its cost.

The far-reaching reforms in Greater London stand out in vivid contrast to the timid and half-hearted attempts to modify the structure in the rest of Britain. In dealing with the metropolitan problem the Government ignored the local authority associations and set up a Royal Commission consisting of persons of independent outlook and unusual ability to inquire into the needs of London Government, without any statutory limitations, Ministerial regulations or other restrictions on their powers and procedure. The Government dealt with the Royal Commission's report on its merits, and embarked on further inquiries only in regard to the composition of the London boroughs. They then drafted the London Government Bill and secured its passage through Parliament.

In dealing with the rest of England, on the other hand, the Government first permitted, then encouraged and later participated in long-drawn-out negotations between the local authority associations about what they would be willing to accept. Having secured agreement involving the very minimum of possible change, the Government then set up the Local Government Commission fettered by an elaborate procedure which weights the scale heavily against reforms of substance. Sir Keith Joseph, the Conservative Minister of Housing and Local Government, was even ready to reject such obvious and moderate proposals as the merging of Rutland with Leicester-shire or the creation of an overspill authority in the West Midlands Special Review Area.

It is obvious that any far-reaching reform, however necessary in the interests of good local government or even to its mere survival, will be opposed tooth and nail by the local authorities concerned. It can, in fact, only be brought about by the action of the Central government, acting on its own initiative.

XXXII

PLAIN SPEAKING BY Mr CROSSMAN

Mr Crossman, in an address to the Association of Municipal Corporations at their Torquay Conference in September 1965, spoke more plainly than any Minister of Housing and Local Government had ever done before about the present state of local government. He began by saying that the once friendly though indifferent attitude of the public towards local government had given way to one of resentful disillusionment. The basic cause of this distrust is that 'the whole structure of local government is out of date, that our county boroughs and county councils as at present organized are archaic institutions, whose size and structure make them increasingly ill-adapted to fulfilling the immensely important functions with which they are charged. The greatest obstacle, in fact, which prevents efficient councils from retaining public confidence is the obsolete constitutional framework within which they have to operate.' He warned councillors and officials that they would have to accept the unpleasant truth that drastic reforms could not be indefinitely postponed without the danger of a breakdown.

Mr Crossman went on to say that effective planning is impossible at present owing to the cold war between local authorities, their undersized areas, and the impossibility of providing enough qualified planners to meet the needs of 150 local planning authorities. Water supply and water resources, the police forces, transport and traffic regulation, all present problems which cannot be solved within the existing framework of local government.

The Local Government Commission, said the Minister, is prevented by its terms of reference from producing the reorganization of local government that we so desperately need. He deplored the appllingly slow and time-wasting procedures laid down by the 1958 Act, and the way in which they have been deliberately exploited in order to frustrate change. Nonetheless, he thought the Commission could still do useful work and he intended to allow it to continue, although he had been tempted to replace it by a new Commission with clear instructions about the changes at which it should aim. The obstacle to such a course is that there are at present no 'accepted principles of reorganization; no established doctrine according to which a Commission could proceed to reshape the areas and the functions of local government so as to enable it to do its job in modern terms and to regain the public confidence that has been lost'. He therefore believed it would be necessary to appoint first a 'powerful and impartial committee' to work out a general policy on which the Commission's terms of reference and directives could be based. This policy would emerge from an authoritative analysis of the two main problems: namely the relation of size to function, and the relation of local democracy to efficiency. The work of this hypothetical committee, he postulated, would be of such overwhelming validity that 'its analysis would be accepted as established doctrine by both sides in the conflict'.

These were brave and challenging words; and they must have been highly unpalatable to the participants in the conference. But Mr Crossman is doomed to severe disappointment if he imagines that the local authority associations, which are defence organizations of the most pronounced type, would accept any analysis by any committee he or anyone else might appoint, if its recommendations threatened the interests or the existence of their members.

Fundamental reform is in any case likely to be effected not by speeches at conferences, but by clear thinking at Ministerial and Departmental level, and above all by political drive and legislative and administrative follow-up. The only action indicated by Mr Crossman in his Torquay speech was the appointment of a Committee to tell him what he is to tell another Commission to do. This is scarcely likely to produce the rapid action which he rightly desires.

Furthermore, if the powers and procedures of the present Local Government Commission are inadequate to solve the larger problems which confront local government—as they certainly are—it is surely wrong to allow it to continue, since its proceedings take up an immense amount of time and energy on the part of councillors, aldermen, and the chief officers of local authorities—not to mention the members and staff of the Commission itself. Shortly after Mr Crossman's speech, the Commission announced it would itself suspend operations.

While, therefore, we may applaud the substance of the Minister's speech and the candour which inspired it, the wisdom of making such an onslaught in the absence of a clear policy of reform with which to back it up, is less evident. It is, however, refreshing to have some plain words from a responsible Minister in place of the deadly soothing syrup to which we have been accustomed for so long.

XXXIII

CONCLUSIONS

I have discussed at some length in these pages the reorganization of the local government structure. My reason for so doing is that this is fundamental to the survival of local government, and it is a matter on which immediate action is now supposed to be impending, after an unduly long period of inaction.

It is, however, not the only aspect of local government which is in urgent need of reform. As I have shown, the relations of central and local government are far from satisfactory, and in particular local authorities have become much too dependent on Exchequer grants and without adequate sources of local revenue. Local authorities have become subservient to the central government, mainly but not entirely because of their excessive dependence on central grants.

The relations of central and local government should rest on the following principles:

(1) It is the responsibility of the central government to see that the organization of local government is well adapted to the functions it is required to perform and the role it is expected to fulfil. By organization I mean the status, areas, powers resources and relations of local authorities.

(2) The central government, in conjunction with Parliament, should formulate the broad lines of policy which local authorities are to follow in respect of the major services.

(3) The major services should be subject to inspection by the Central Departments concerned in order to ensure the attainment of a national minimum standard. This applies to the police, housing, highways, fire protection, health, education and welfare.

(4) The Central Departments should act as clearing houses

149

of information and provide technical advice to local authorities. For this purpose they should develop their own research and information services to a much higher level than has hitherto been attained.[1]

(5) Exchequer grants should be provided either in respect of the main services or as a method of supplementing local sources of taxation; but the total subventions thus received should not exceed the sums obtained by local authorities from their own sources of taxation, as they are now doing in many areas. When the ratio of grants to local taxes is greater than 40 : 60 the local authority is in a position of dangerous subordination.

(6) There is a need to concede much greater freedom to local authorities to strike out in new directions as they think fit.

In conclusion, I must reaffirm my belief in the virtues of a sound and healthy system of local self-government. Few people today appear to understand the essential role of local government in the welfare state. I cannot comprehend how a society can call itself a welfare state unless it strived to ensure the widest possible participation by the citizens in the exercise of political power and the making of executive decisions. Local government is the best possible instrument to distribute power widely on democratic lines.

Today, unfortunately, there is a strong tendency in this country and elsewhere to concentrate power at the centre to an excessive degree and to neglect the potentialities of local government. As a consequence we are in some danger of becoming a managerial society, with the levers of power in the hands of an elite which manages private industry and trade through giant commercial companies, runs nationalized industries through public corporations, and public administration through a civil service working in the shadows of the Ministers whose powers they exercise.

Only by a three-pronged attack on organization, finance and central-local relations can we give local government its proper

---

[1] See my *Governors and the Governed* (1964), chapter 2, on the whole question of communication and the provision of good intelligence and information services.

CONCLUSIONS

place in our polity. Only thus can we preserve and strengthen the qualities of local initiative, civic pride and public spirit from which the political virtues of the nation have sprung. Only thus can we develop and enhance the sense of community upon which a genuine democracy must rest.

INDEX

Economic Planning Boards and
Councils, *see* 'Regionalism'
Education, 16, 26, 78, 86, 114, 117
Made a function of County
Councils, 33, 34, 126
Delegation, 33, 35–6, 38, 102,
103, 140
Central Control, 48, 50–1, 149
Finance, 66
Further Education, 74, 112, 123,
127, 129, 132
in London, 138, 140–1
and Regionalism, 42, 129, 131,
132
Education and Science, Department
of, 35, 36, 49–52
Electricity Supply, 21–3, 25, 26,
27, 47, 87, 136
Area Boards, 22, 23, 136
Electricity Council, 22, 23
Entertainment, 30–2, 132, 139
Tax on, 55, 62, 67, 68
Essex, 138
Eston, 135
Excepted Districts, 33, 35–6, 37,
103, 140
Exeter, 116
Expenditure of Local Authorities,
Total, 53
Eye, 71

Fabian Society, 26–7, 132
Finance of Local Govt., 53–68, 79,
97–8, 123, 149–50, 151
New Sources of, 55–6, 59–60,
64–5, 67–8
The Free Penny, 63
1957 White Paper, 55–6, 61–2,
63, 64
see also 'Grants' and 'Rates'
Fire Service, 74, 117
Made a function of County
Councils, 33, 34, 126
Central Control of, 48, 149
in London, 139, 142
Reform Proposals, 87, 103, 112,
123, 127, 131, 132

Flintshire, 121
Flood Prevention, 129
Food and Drugs, 38, 87, 140
Functions of Local Authorities, 85,
105–8, 111, 149
and Regionalism, 43–5, 133
Gains, 29–32
Losses, 13–25, 79–80, 109
1957 White Paper, 37–9, 100
Importance of size for effectiveness, 72–3, 102, 125, 127, 147
in London, 139–41
Changes within Local Govt.,
33–40, 109
in Wales, 121–2, 123
see also 'Delegation', 'London',
'Special Review Areas' and
under individual functions

Gas Supply, 23–4, 26, 27, 47, 87,
136
Gateshead, 113
General Review Areas, 114–16,
117–18, *see also* 'Local Govt.
Commission'
Glamorganshire, 70, 121
Gloucester, 71, 116
Grants
Local dependence on, 53–68,
109, 149–50
Block, 17, 47, 48, 51
General, 48, 56, 61, 62, 64, 65,
66
Percentage, 48, 51, 56, 62, 64
Exchequer Equalisation, 17, 56,
57, 64
Rate Deficiency, 17, 57, 61, 66,
121
Greater London, *see* 'London'
Great Yarmouth, 116
Grimsby, 116

Hart, Sir Wm., 48, 120, 133–4
Hastings, 94
Health, Ministry of, 14, 39, 47, 49,
51, 78, 82, 83; *see also* 'Bevan,
Mr. Aneurin'